Canada Our History

An Album Through Time

Rick Archbold

Doubleday Canada
an Otherwise Inc. Edition

Canadian Cataloguing in Publication Data

Archbold, Rick, 1950–
    Canada – our history : an album through time

ISBN 0-385-25971-9

1. Canada — History — 20th century — Pictorial works.
2. Canada — History — 20th century. I. Title.

FC600.A722000   971'.0022'2   C00-931317-6
F1034.2.A722000

Printed and bound in Great Britain

Produced by Otherwise Inc. Editions
356A Queen Street West
Toronto, Ontario
 M5V 2A2

Published in Canada by Doubleday Canada,
a division of Random House of Canada Limited

BT   10   9   8   7   6   5   4   3   2   1

Canada: Our History was produced by Otherwise Inc. Editions
Editorial direction and art direction Sara Borins
Graphic design Concrete Design Communications Inc. (Toronto)
Editor Karen Alliston
Editorial assistance and research Tom Berkhout, Jennifer Heyns,
Sarah Webster

Otherwise Inc. Editions offers special thanks to Anne-Marie Beaton,
Derek Berkhout, Dean Cooke, Catherine Dean, Andrea Gordon,
Christine Innes, Martha Kanya-Forstner, Rick Feldman, Diti Katona,
Janine Laporte, Jerry Levitan, Brad Martin, Maya Mavjee,
John Pearce, John Pylypczak, Peter Jacobsen, Lou Ann Sartori,
Derek Shapton, Henry Tyminski

Author's acknowledgements
Like all books, this one was created by a team, but putting together
Canada: Our History involved more than the usual amount of
teamwork. Several people helped me track down sources or experts:
Kathryn Dean; Alex Fischer; Nancy Flight; Faye Katzman; Alistair
MacKay. Almost every chapter is more real and more accurate
because someone helped by providing information, or checking over
what I'd written, or both. Thanks go to: Ross Kakwirakeron
Montour ("Trouble at Oka"); John Ibbitson ("Hurricane Hazel");
Ward McBurney ("Hurricane Hazel"); Ken Moy ("Canada Wins!");
Christopher Needles ("Millennium Trip"); Andrew Podnieks
("Canada Wins!"); Floyd St. Clair ("Off to War"); Daniel Sanger
("Guns in October"); Don Ward ("Starting Over"); David Watmough
("Off to War"). These people read the entire book for accuracy:
Joy Cohnstaedt; Susan Haines; Christopher Moore; Morris Wolfe.
The errors that remain are mine alone, but there are many fewer
of them because of the tireless and enthusiastic fact-checking of
Jennifer Heyns.

    Last but not least, a big thank you to the people who guided
this book from concept to finished product: Alison Maclean, who
made editorial comments on some of the chapters; Tom Berkhout
at Otherwise, who helped with production and photo research;
editor and copy editor Karen Alliston, whose sensitive and acute
queries and suggestions always hit home; Sara Borins of Otherwise,
who had the idea in the first place, who never let me forget our
goal, and who expertly saw the whole project through from start to
finish; and Henry Tyminski of Concrete Design who gave this
book its beautiful design.

This book is dedicated to Rick Feldman, without whom none of it
would have been half as much fun.

17

101

131

65

111

47

75

Contents

57

93

139

149

27

121

37

83

Preface

Writing *Canada: Our History* has been a lot of fun. More fun than I could have imagined. When I was a kid, Canadian history seemed dull compared to the history of other countries. I was a lot more interested in the stories of King Arthur and his Round Table or the battles of the American Civil War or the explorers who ventured into "darkest" Africa than I was in the story of good old Canada, my home and native land. Maybe the history that's nearest always seems less exciting. At least at first glance. Once you take a closer look, however, it becomes a lot more interesting.

This book is about taking a closer look at some of the adventures Canadians have lived through during the last hundred years. But instead of telling these stories the way they do in textbooks, mostly through the eyes of adults, we've chosen to tell them through the eyes of the kids who were there. Who saw and felt what happened. Whose lives were changed forever. Each of the stories in this book narrates a piece of Canadian history as it might have been experienced by someone between the ages of ten and seventeen.

Notice that in the previous sentence I used the word *might*. The kids in this book are made up, but the events they experience are real. So, when you read "The Day the World Ended," the story of the Halifax Explosion, the facts are as accurate as I could make them even if the person who's telling the story and his nephew Tom are people I've invented. Although it's true that more than 10,000 people were killed or injured because of the explosion, I don't know if a five-year-old named Tom was one of them.

When I say the main characters in these stories are made up, that's not entirely true. Many of them are based on someone I know or on stories I've heard or read. My friend Ken Moy, for example, who grew up in Vancouver's Chinatown in the 1950s, gave me the idea for the boy in the story "Canada Wins!" But Ken wasn't a hockey fan, and by the time of the Canada-Soviet 1972 hockey summit he was in college. However, his parents did grow bean sprouts in the bathtub, so that part is true. My niece Jennifer Macdonald, who wasn't even born in 1967, would definitely have had as good a time at Expo 67 in Montreal as the narrator of "Grooving at Expo." Too bad she missed it. I loved Expo and used the memories of my own visit to help me imagine what it would have been like for the two girls in the story. The book comes closest to my personal experience when it covers the period when I was a kid – the 1960s. So I could have been the boy standing on Parliament Hill with his parents and grandmother in "Fighting Over a Flag," and wanting to be somewhere else – anywhere else. But I definitely didn't know enough about the Internet to have written "Millennium Trip" without the help of my personal e-mail chat guru, Christopher Needles, who also happens to be – very loosely – the inspiration for one of the two kids in the story.

Writing *Canada: Our History* gave me a chance to play fifteen different roles, to pretend to be fifteen different kids living in Canada at fifteen different times. I hope that when you read these stories you'll do the same thing, imagine what it was like to be there. What it was like to taste and smell and feel Canadian history.

Our history is as varied and exciting as any history anywhere. I know. Because now I've been there.

Rick Archbold

Introduction

Click! Maybe it's a camera in a cardboard carton from the drugstore. You're going to toss it when the film's developed. Or *click*, you're using a Polaroid. In a few seconds you'll be laughing with the gang at what you just shot.

Maybe, click, it's a digital. You can e-mail the pictures to your cousins or put them up on that Web site. Could be the family camcorder – *dzzzzz*. Maybe, *click*, *bzzz*, you signed out that mega-bucks, motor-driven, high-performance, single-lens-reflex from the photo club. Got a telephoto lens and an exposure meter and a tripod. You might be in the darkroom half the night developing prints for the photo contest.

Kids and pictures. Kids have been taking pictures for a long time. It was 1900, exactly 1900, when the Kodak company produced a little camera called the "Brownie." The Brownie was the first camera for everybody.

A Brownie cost a dollar. The film cost fifteen cents for six exposures. "Can be operated by any schoolboy or girl," boasted the Kodak Company. And millions of kids showed it was true. Brownie cameras were around forever. Kodak sold them until 1970. That old snap of your grandparents, the one with the curled-up white borders and the scalloping around the edges, that would have been taken with a Brownie.

A hundred years of everybody snapping pictures! Think of all the pictures we have. Stored on the hard drive. Racked up in the VCR. Stuck up in the kitchen with a fridge magnet. In a push-pin collage on your bedroom bulletin board. Printed on a T-shirt. Sitting on your mother's desk in a frame you made back in daycamp. Baby pictures all over grandma's place. All those class photos you sit for every year.

11

A few of your pictures get into the photo album. But if you're like me, mostly they're heaped in shoeboxes, or up on the high shelf of the back closet. Just once in a while, maybe you're spring cleaning, or you're moving, or maybe some old relative died, and somebody pulls out the box of memories.

I love looking at old photographs. Sometimes I love looking at old photographs because they're so familiar – "Hey, I'd forgotten that!" or maybe "Yeah, that must be Uncle Peter as a kid. He changed, but that's him for sure."

Just as often, I like old pictures because they're so strange. Look at the way they wore their hair! Imagine getting around in cars like that! What if you had to work in a kitchen like that one? (Or an office. Or a factory. Or a field of wheat.) Why do they stand up so straight, ties knotted, hats on?

There's a time machine in an old photograph. Photographs let us look into worlds of the past.

But when you travel in time, you find you don't know where you are any more. Look at that old photograph for more than a moment, and you really start to wonder. Why did they do it that way? What were they thinking? *Who were they, anyway?* Look at that old photograph for more than a moment. It starts more questions than it answers. There's a mystery in every one.

In this book, Rick Archbold has looked at some old photographs of Canada. (Some go back to the time when Brownie cameras were new.) He's found that it's true: every picture really is worth a thousand words. It takes at least that many words to sort out what's really going on in each picture.

Look at those two little girls in white aprons in a circle of passengers aboard the immigrant ship. Wouldn't it take at least a thousand words to imagine where they come from, where they might get to, what they dream of as they pass the time and the ship heaves through the Atlantic rollers? *Who are they?*

Look at those kids' eyes, the kids in Halifax, when was that, 1917? They had an explosion, sure. But what did kids say who survived that? What could they have told us about how the city came apart? How did they live through it when so many people didn't? *What were they thinking?*

Look at that hockey player, the guy with the maple leaf on his shirt and the big happy look in his eyes. Okay, it's a hockey picture, he's scored a goal. What is it that makes your uncles go crazy: "Hey, the '72 series! I remember exactly…," and start reciting the play-by-play? *Why are some pictures so powerful to some people?*

Rick Archbold has looked at a lot of photographs of Canada. He's wondered about the mysteries inside those time machines. He's asked himself those who-what-why questions.

In these pages, he's tried to answer them. How it felt to be amid the clash of strikers and mounted policemen along the streetcar lines of Winnipeg. To get caught up in the Quint craze in Ontario. To send your dad off to war, maybe forever. These aren't the only "answers" to the questions the pictures raise. Just *an* answer.

But try these answers out. See if they don't send you back to the photographs that started them off. Probably with more questions!

This is our country. This is our history. We all took these pictures. Now we all get to share them.

Christopher Moore   **13**

Starting Over

April 30, 1905
Dear Ruth,

TOMORROW WE LAND IN CANADA, AT THE GREAT PORT city of Quebec. For the first time in days everybody on board this crowded old ship seems to be in a good mood. This afternoon the weather was mild enough that most of the passengers in steerage – that's the word they use for the cheapest and stinkiest part of the ship! – came up on deck. One of the women even began dancing, and everyone gathered around. It looked nothing like the dances you and I do together, but it made me feel homesick for our village anyway.

Mama and baby Zygmund have been seasick for most of the time since we left the port city of Hamburg nearly two weeks ago. With the five of us crammed into one small, dingy cabin, we barely get any sleep. One night I woke up to Mama's screaming. A big rat was sitting on her bed staring at her! After her scream, the rat decided he'd rather visit a quieter cabin.

Your best friend,
Dora

17

An early twentieth-century Quebec City streetscape shows a street paved with wooden boards.

May 1, 1905

Dear Ruth,

I'm writing this from the city of Quebec, where our ship just landed. Quebec looks a lot like cities back home, except that it isn't as big and it isn't as old. I expected everything in Canada to be bigger and better, but it isn't. Some of the streets are paved with cobbles or even wood! Some are just dirt. When it rains, they turn to mud.

It is very strange not being able to understand a word people say. After we got off the ship we were crowded like cattle into a huge building with a very high ceiling. We waited for hours until the immigration official could talk to us. And then he didn't speak our language. But at least he let us all pass through the gate.

I'll write you a longer letter from the train, which leaves tonight. My papa says we will be voyaging as far across land as we've come across water. Maybe even farther.

Your best friend,

Dora

A Canadian government photographer took this portrait of a newly arrived immigrant family at the Quebec City wharf in 1905.

18

May 15, 1905
Dear Ruth,

We arrived in Saskatoon a few days ago. We have to wait here until Papa gets the grant for our land. We are living in a city of tents at the edge of town. It may be almost summer back home, but here it is hard to describe the season. One minute it is hot and the next minute it is cold. When it's hot, the biting insects are terrible. Little Eva's whole body is covered with welts.

We arrived here by train from Quebec and Regina. There must have been about thirty families packed into each train car. The Canadians call them Colonist Cars, I guess because they are taking us to "colonize" the West. Day after day we sat on hard benches and watched the rocks and lakes and forests passing by the window. You cannot imagine how great the distances are between the towns.

How often did this primitive mailbox get mail? Not often. Regular rural mail delivery didn't reach the prairies until the 1920s. Before that, farmers had to drive into town to pick up the mail.

Then one morning the trees disappeared. In every direction, nothing. I had no idea the sky could be so big. It took my breath away. One person seems very small here. I want to hear about everything that's happening back home. Write to me soon.

Your best friend,
Dora

This picture of a Colonist Car shows how it could be converted into a dormitory. You paid $3 to rent bedding: a mattress, curtains, blankets, and a pillow.

October 1, 1905

Dear Ruth,

We only had to wait a few more days before Papa received his "quarter section" from the government Land Office in Saskatoon. (A quarter section is 160 acres, about three times the size of a typical farm back home.) We spent the rest of our savings on everything we would need to start our farm: seed for planting, a horse for pulling the plough, a cow for milking, and six chickens for laying eggs. Then we had to travel by road – if you could call it that – more than sixty miles to the southwest to the town of Rosetown, which is the nearest place of any size to our land.

This man has waited all night outside the Dominion Land Office in Regina to be first in line to buy a quarter section (160 acres). The land grant cost $10.

The fall harvest was a community event. When the privately owned steam-powered threshing machine came into an area, the local farmers co-operated to get the threshing done as quickly and cheaply as possible.

To call Rosetown a town would be like calling our swimming pond back home a lake. It has about ten buildings along a main street: a hotel, a hardware store and a general store, a few houses. That's all.

You can't imagine how lonely I felt when we finally arrived at our land, which is about five miles outside of town. There was nothing there. Our "farm" was a flat piece of prairie that had never been touched by a plough. The nearest settlers were more than a mile away and they weren't from back home. We lived in a big tent while we planted our first crop of wheat. We all pitched in to help, Mama, Papa, even Eva. Our nearest neighbours helped as soon as they had finished their own crop. I've never been so tired in my life. And once the planting was done, we had to think about someplace more permanent to live.

There are almost no trees here, so we built our house out of sod. Can you believe it? We cut one-foot-square pieces of prairie sod with the grass still growing on them and used them as bricks. Once the walls were built, we placed poplar poles across the top – we have a few poplar trees growing by the stream that runs through our property – and then covered the poles with more sod. That's our roof! The floor is hard-packed mud and the walls inside are whitewashed. After the first heavy rain, the roof dripped for days. I wonder what it will be like during the winter.

Your best friend,
Dora

As soon as they could afford to, the settlers replaced their sod houses with ones made of wood, like the log house pictured here.

Going up ...

The first decade of the century was a time of settling and building. Canada's population exploded in the century's first decade, growing from five million in 1901 to seven million in 1911. In the cities, new buildings seemed to rise every day. In the countryside, new railroad tracks were laid and new roads built. Among the most important and impressive structures were the bridges being built to span Canada's great rivers. Work began on the first Quebec Bridge, pictured below, in 1900. When completed, it would be the longest steel cantilever bridge in the world and would provide the first year-round link between the Quebec City and the south shore of the St. Lawrence River.

This family scene was undoubtedly posed for a government brochure promoting pioneer life.

May 1, 1906

Dear Ruth,

Our sod house was warm enough once winter came, but we hadn't counted on the snow. One morning the snow started, and it didn't stop all day. When we went to bed it was still snowing and the wind was howling.

The next morning, when I tried to get outside so I could go to the outhouse, our front door wouldn't open. My papa came over and gave it a shove. Nothing. Then Mama and I helped. The door moved about an inch.

Eva started to wail: "We're trapped, we're going to die." Then baby Zygmund started to scream. Papa stayed

Since there were no refrigerators, the settlers cut blocks of ice from frozen ponds and rivers to keep food cool.

... and Falling Down

On a June day in 1907, the partially completed Quebec Bridge collapsed into the St. Lawrence River, killing seventy-five workers. This was only one of many accidents and disasters in the early years of the century. The country was building so fast that sometimes the builders got careless. The collapse of the Quebec Bridge was one of the worst work-related disasters. Before the bridge was finally completed in 1917, it collapsed yet again, killing ten more men. Several other workers died during the construction in other accidents. So the first Quebec Bridge took seventeen years to build and cost more than eighty-five lives.

calm, but Mama began crying quietly. Tears were streaming down her face but she hardly made a sound. I hadn't seen her cry once since the day we left our home village. That day, when she hugged her sister goodbye, she just sobbed and sobbed. This crying was much worse.

It turned out that the snow was up to the roof of our house and the wind had packed it hard against our door. No one had told us that around here you never make a door that opens outward, because the snow can lock you in. Fortunately, our closest neighbours came by to dig us out!

Your best friend,
Dora

October 1, 1907
Dear Ruth,

When we arrived here there was nothing. Now there are fields of wheat and farmhouses with neat vegetable gardens and a church. Grass is growing on our sod roof!

Last spring, after the planting was done, all the neighbours for miles around gathered to build a brand-new schoolhouse. It was finished in three days! My English is improving – I'm even learning to write it. But at home we all speak our own language because Mama and Papa just can't learn.

Eva, who's now nine, is in school, too. All the grades are together in the same room and our teacher has to teach us all at once. My best friend at school is a girl our age. She just turned fourteen. Her name is Margaret and she comes from Scotland and speaks English with an accent that's even funnier than mine. Remember when I told you how we had to get dug out of our house? It was Margaret's family who helped us. Do you think you will ever come to Canada to visit us?
Your friend,
Dora

In schools outside of cities, grades one to eight shared a single room and one teacher. As one settler remembered, "I never quite knew what I was studying. I was mostly listening to other kids reading, since there never was a moment of quietness."

Rushing for Riches

While boatloads of immigrants from Europe came to the Canadian west, hundreds of thousands of others were heading to Canada's Yukon, where gold had been discovered in 1896. Most of those who came looking for instant riches were Americans. And most of them went home poorer than when they arrived.

These men are hiking from Skagway in the Alaskan panhandle over the White Pass into the Yukon. An arduous trek at the best of times, winter blizzards could turn the pass into a cold, white nightmare.

This is one of the more than sixty steamboats that sailed the Klondike River during the height of the gold rush, carrying people and supplies to the town of Dawson, briefly the largest settlement north of Seattle.

A few prospectors did strike it very rich. Here is some of the gold that was dug from Yukon soil – more than half a million dollars worth in gold bars.

Far more men than women joined the Klondike gold rush, but as the town of Dawson boomed, more women arrived. Here, two of them try their hand at panning for gold.

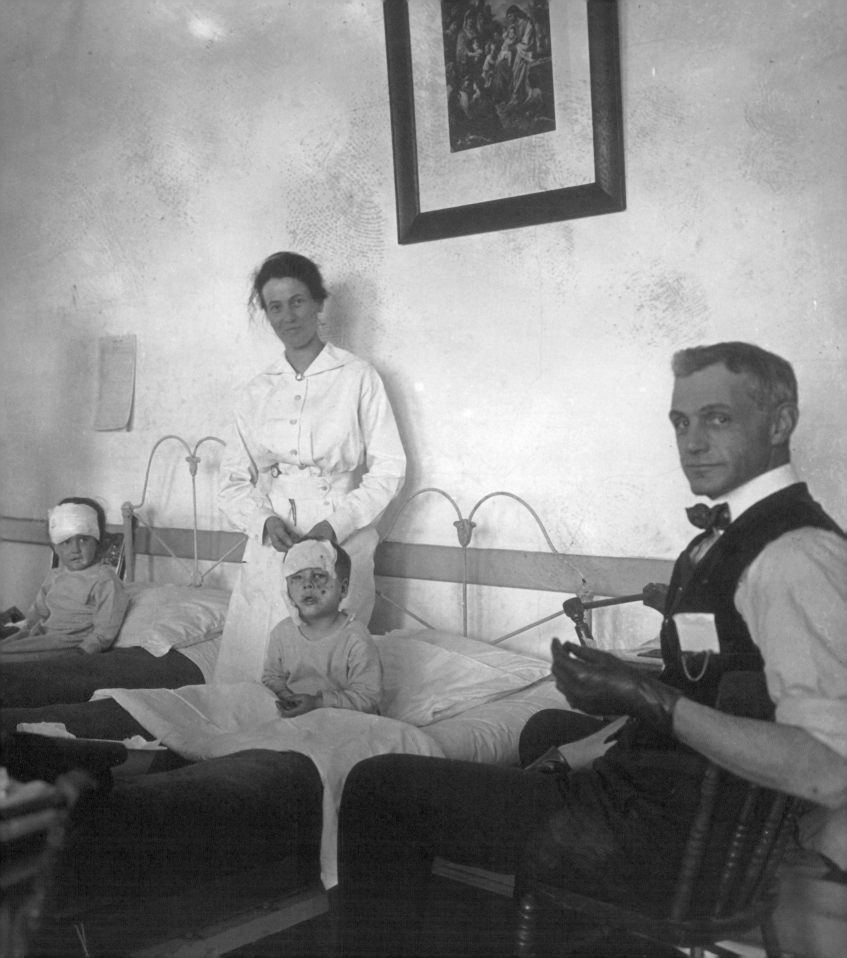

The Day the World Ended

WHEN I LOOKED AT TOM, I THOUGHT TO MYSELF, "Our world has ended." On December 6, 1917, during the disaster called the Halifax Explosion, five-year-old Tom lost both his sight and his power of speech. That afternoon, when I found him in the Camp Hill Hospital, the doctors told me there was still a chance his eyesight would return. I doubted, however, that he would speak again. Tom looked as though the words had simply been blasted right out of him. It was a miracle that he was alive at all.

Tom is my nephew. He was but one of thousands upon thousands of people in Halifax and Dartmouth, Nova Scotia, who suffered terrible injuries in the worst explosion human beings would manage to create until the detonation of the first atomic bomb nearly thirty years later. This is my story of the Halifax Explosion.

My last look at Halifax the way I had always known it came early on the morning of December 6 as I walked home long before sunrise. My job in the newsroom at the Halifax *Herald* kept me up all night. Because of the war against Germany, those of us too young to fight held jobs that usually went to older men. In 1917, I was seventeen years old. Thanks to me and my work-mates, Haligonians awoke each morning to find the latest news about the war crisply folded and neatly placed on their doorsteps.

Nineteenth-century cannons on the site of the Halifax Citadel still seemed to guard the city.

As this Halifax family portrait shows, Canadian families used to be much bigger than they are today.

I arrived home well before the sun rose. I lived alone in those days. Thank God my parents were safe and sound in the house in Truro where I'd lived until I was sixteen. A few hours later, I awoke to find my bed shaking violently, as if from an earthquake.

My first thought was, "The Germans are attacking the city!" Above me, I heard pots and pans crashing to the floor. At the same time I heard an almost musical tinkling. I soon realized that the noise was the shattering of glass. Then I thought of my sister Isabel and young Tom.

Were they all right?

I dressed in a frenzy and ran up the stairs. The contents of the kitchen cupboards werc strewn everywhere along with shards of broken glass. When I stepped out the gaping front door, which swung on its hinges, I thought at first that it was raining. But when I held out my hand to catch the drops, I discovered they were black. A black rain was falling. (Later I learned this was an oily soot created by the carbon that had not been fully burned in the explosion.) It stuck to my face and clothing almost like liquid tar. In the distance, I could see flames flickering among the houses

These two teacups survived the blast, while some stone buildings collapsed into rubble.

higher up on the hillside. I thought to myself, "This must be what the battle-fields of France look like." That made me cast my mind across the sea to my older brother, James, who was an infantryman

The day after the explosion, snow fell on the harbour. The Imo, *the ship that caused the blast, can be seen near the far shore.*

Parts of downtown Halifax looked like they'd been bombed. The explosion left thousands of people homeless.

stuck somewhere in a muddy trench in France. Then my brotherly instincts took over: Find Isabel and Tom!

I shudder to recount the sight that met my eyes when I reached my sister's house in Richmond. Like all the others in this district, perched on a hillside with nothing between them and the full force of the blast, it lay in smoking ruins. I approached her neighbour, who stood nearby looking dazed and helpless. He told me that she and Tom had only just now been taken by ambulance to the hospital down by the harbour. And so I continued my dreadful errand.

Most of the buildings downtown were still standing, although some had lost their roofs, but the streets were choked with debris among which wounded people wandered like living ghosts. The city, devoid as it was of the ordinary sounds of vehicles and machinery, had taken on a supernatural silence.

The closer I came to the harbour, the worse the damage and the carnage became. Wounded men, women, and children lay dying in the street. Some of those already lifeless appeared not to have a scratch on them. Some of the living had injuries too awful to describe. Later reports put the total number of dead or wounded at more than 10,000.

The harbour itself was a blasted wasteland. Across the Narrows on the Dartmouth shore I could make out the blazing hulk of a freighter. I later learned that this sorry wreck was the

Imo, the Belgian relief ship that had accidentally set off the entire disaster.

Just before 9:00 a.m., while I was still soundly sleeping but while most of Halifax was already up and starting its day, a French munitions ship, the *Mont Blanc*, loaded with explosives, entered the Narrows on its way into the harbour. Meanwhile, the *Imo*, preparing to exit the harbour, had temporarily stopped its engines so as to avoid hitting a passing barge. But when the barge had passed, the *Imo* found itself bearing down on the steaming *Mont Blanc*, and was unable to turn away in time.

The collision was slight, but the friction of metal hull on metal hull sent sparks flying. These sparks ignited one of the barrels of benzine being carried on deck, which ignited the next and the next until the fire spread to the explosives stored below. The resulting conflagration blew the ship to kingdom come. The enormous explosion launched a tidal wave

A few of those still left on board survived. The ship's pilot was killed, but the helmsman escaped with only a badly broken leg.

Armed guards keep watch over the Imo, *the ship that set off the explosion and was then thrown against the Dartmouth shore.*

News of Disaster

Before television and radio, the only way people got the news was from the newspaper. As a result, newspapers flourished. Most cities had three or four dailies; many smaller towns had more than one. Competition between them was fierce, especially to be the first to report the big news items, like wars and disasters. As the country grew, there were lots of disasters to report, including the Moose River Mine Disaster of 1936, during which three men were buried alive in a collapsed gold mine near Moose River, Nova Scotia. The headline below celebrates the rescue of two of these three after being trapped for sixty-nine hours.

that drowned many people on shore, unleashed a deadly rain of molten metal on the city, and caused a shock wave that did damage all the way to Truro, more than fifty miles away. (My mother later told me that her kitchen window had collapsed onto the table where she and my father had been sitting only moments before.)

Most of the men aboard the *Mont Blanc* abandoned ship before the blazing deck detonated the explosive cargo, but one straggler was lifted in the explosion's cyclone and deposited, nearly naked, on a nearby hillside. Miraculously, he was unharmed. Not so lucky were the fire boats that had swarmed out from shore to attend to what they believed was nothing more than a burning ship.

I found young Tom in the hospital where many of the injured had been taken, but of my sister's fate I could learn nothing. Men, women, and children of all sorts and classes were literally packed in the wards like sardines in a box. The cots were all occupied, and

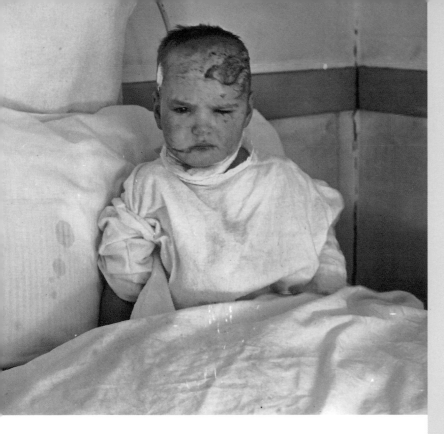

This survivor of the explosion could be young Tom: badly injured but still alive and likely to recover.

Big Bangs

Big as it was, the Halifax Explosion was a pipsqueak compared to the detonation of a hydrogen bomb, like the one below being exploded during a test in a remote part of the Pacific Ocean. Most of the immediate damage when a bomb goes off is caused by the concussion wave, or shock wave, it creates. In the Halifax Explosion, the concussion wave knocked down whole buildings. When the first atomic bombs were dropped on the Japanese cities of Hiroshima and Nagasaki, these two cities were flattened. But nuclear explosions also have a horrible after-effect: poisonous radioactive fallout whose damage may take years to appear.

the floors covered so that it was often difficult to step between them. Since Tom could not speak I couldn't ask him where his mother could be found. I didn't need to ask Tom where his father was. Like my brother, he was in Europe fighting the Germans.

The heavy snow that fell on Halifax that night settled like a dreadful shroud. The air had turned to a more seasonal December cold, and all over the city Haligonians huddled beneath blankets in their unheated cellars, as far as they could get from their gaping windows.

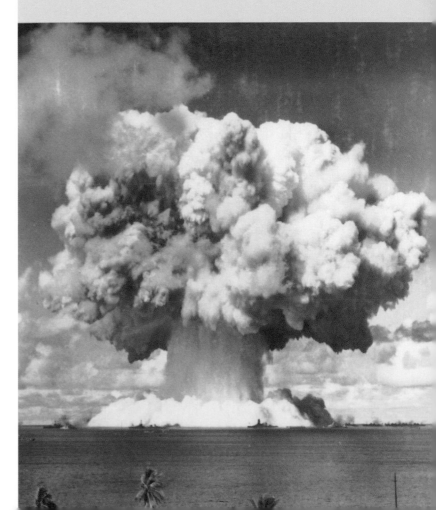

Mourners gather at a mass funeral for those killed in the Halifax Explosion. In all, the blast claimed 1,600 lives and injured a further 9,000, two hundred of them blinded by flying glass. Six thousand people were left homeless.

The next day they would begin the long, sad task of finding and burying the dead, including my dear Isabel.

Tom had been found lying in her lifeless arms among the rubble of their modest house. Her body had shielded his.

In the days that followed, I attended more funerals than I can count. The *Herald* building had survived the blast and we managed to get the paper out on December 7. The headline read SCENES AT MORGUES AND HOSPITALS THAT BAFFLE DESCRIPTION. I'm happy to tell you that people began to rebuild the city and that Tom did eventually regain his speech, although he never regained his sight. He had survived the Halifax Explosion of 1917, but the world we had known had ended for good.

The Faraway War

The Halifax Explosion was when World War I came home to the people of Halifax. For the first time they could understand what it was like for the hundreds of thousands of Canadian soldiers who were fighting in France and Belgium against the armies of Germany and Austria.

Canadian troops storm out of a trench near Courcerres, France, during a training exercise before being sent to the real trenches. By the end of the war there were more than 600,000 Canadians in uniform.

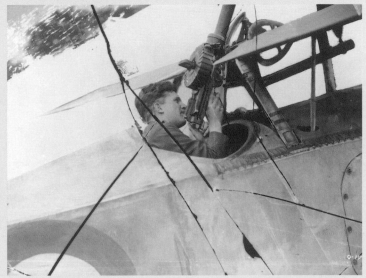

Billy Bishop, who grew up in Owen Sound, Ontario, was Canada's greatest flying ace, with seventy-two enemy planes shot down. One of his fellow pilots called him "a fantastic shot but a terrible pilot."

Canadian soldiers fire big guns before a battle. Canada's famous general, Sir Arthur Currie, always ordered an artillery bombardment before he sent his men in to attack.

A soldier washes in a muddy puddle near the front line. Conditions in the trenches were primitive and many died of diseases contracted in the filthy cold and damp.

Revolution in Winnipeg

FATHER SAYS THAT TODAY, SATURDAY JUNE 21, 1919, will go down as a black day in the history of the Dominion of Canada. This afternoon, the striking workers – what he calls "the scum of Winnipeg" – paraded through the city. According to Father, when the Royal North-West Mounted Police and the special constables tried to get the strikers to disperse, they "behaved like animals." They fought with the Mounties on horseback, and a number of the policemen were injured, and two of the strikers were killed.

"This is a bald-faced attempt at revolution!" Father thundered.

He's been talking that way for weeks. At the beginning I believed him. Now, I'm not so sure. I certainly don't believe that all the strikers are wicked or that more than a few of them want to overthrow the government.

I know these are not proper opinions for a fourteen-year-old girl of my social standing. But then, I've never been a very proper girl – according to my father or my mother.

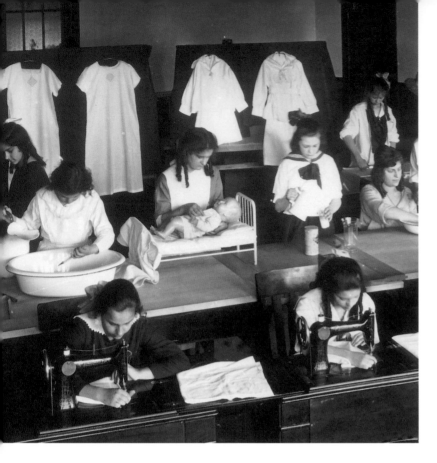

Proper Winnipeg girls, like the ones pictured above, learned the domestic arts, including how to use the sewing machine (first patented in 1844) and how to wash a baby. But for the children of wealthy families, like the girl pictured below, such chores were left to servants who helped them dress and who did their hair.

The General Strike started more than a month ago, but the problems that led to it started a long time before that. After the war ended in November 1918, there were suddenly thousands and thousands of returning soldiers looking for jobs and places to live. Prices soared and working people were getting fed up because they just couldn't seem to make ends meet. In the months before there had been smaller strikes all over western Canada. Everywhere the demands were the same: an eight-hour working day and a decent "living wage."

Thus, when the workers at a few Winnipeg factories walked off the job at 11:00 a.m. on May 15, a lot of other workers were ready to join them. Soon the first strikers were joined by thousands more. Even the Winnipeg police supported the strike, but announced they would stay on the job to keep the peace. By the end of the first day, the whole city had ground to a halt.

We were sent home from Rupert's Land Girls' School shortly after noon. What a relief. I hate that prissy place. Our headmistress is always talking about "the ladylike thing to do" and "a woman's place" till I feel ill. When I told my favourite teacher, Miss Macdonald, that I'd decided to become a doctor, she looked at me somewhat sadly. "Oh, dearie, dearie, me," she said in her soft Scottish brogue. "You won't have an easy time of it, will you, Sara?"

That first evening of the strike, Father announced in no uncertain terms, "None of you is to leave this house without my permission until the strike is over.

There is a real danger of violence."

My brother John – he's a year younger and plans to become a soldier – protested, but Father stood firm. "Sara and John, you will remain under this roof," he said. Standing firm is one of father's specialties. (It's why our secret nickname for him is The General.) He runs an iron foundry and is a colonel in the Winnipeg militia. During the war, he spent all his spare time on the parade ground training soldiers to go overseas.

A year before the strike began, Winnipeggers, like most Canadians, were more concerned with winning the war than labour strife. These Boy Scouts in Regina were raising money to support the war effort.

It was John who suggested that we sneak out of the house and go to the strike rally called for the evening of May 25 in Victoria Park to protest the latest ultimatum to the Winnipeg postal workers: Return to work by 10 a.m. the next day or lose your jobs!

Though John is a year younger, I can fit into his clothes. So it was simple to get myself up as a boy. I wear my hair short – my mother hates it and says she despairs of my ever getting married – so I could hide it completely under a cap. Mother, who is a fragile flower, had retreated to her room as soon as the strike commenced. She wouldn't even know we'd been gone.

It was a lovely spring evening and there were a surprising number of people on the Portage Avenue streetcar. (Although the drivers had joined the strike, replacement drivers had been hired.) It being early June, there was still plenty of daylight by the time we reached Victoria Park, which is near the City Hall. The crowd was very angry.

One of the strike leaders was shouting: "The Citizens' Committee

A strike leader addresses a mass meeting in Victoria Park.

say you must call off the sympathetic strikes. What is your answer?"

As if with one voice, the crowd roared back, "NO!"

Speaker followed speaker, as John and I explored the crowd. Suddenly I felt a gentle tap on my shoulder. It was a young man I recognized who works at Father's foundry. On my occasional visits there, he has always doffed his cap and smiled graciously.

"What on earth are you doing here, Miss Sara?" he asked.

"I've come to see for myself."

"These are not bad people," he continued almost apologetically. "It is simply that we have all had enough of being mistreated by the bosses and paid a starvation wage and not even given the right to form a union and negotiate as a group."

"But Father says you want to start a revolution," I told him.

"Stuff and nonsense," he replied. "We just want to be treated like decent human beings."

I thought about his words as we made our way home.

An anti-Bolshevik demonstration (above) on the steps of Winnipeg City Hall. Many Winnipeggers believed the strikers wanted a revolution like the one led by the Bolsheviks in Russia in 1917. A group of strikers (below) carries a banner condemning scabs, those who have taken jobs held by those on strike. Until the strike turned violent, most of the men stayed off work and out of trouble.

After dispersing a crowd of strikers, these Mounties have dismounted from their horses and are occupying a downtown Winnipeg street.

On June 1, 10,000 soldiers, who'd recently come home from overseas, marched to the provincial legislature and then to City Hall to insist that the government agree to strikers' demands. ("Traitors," my father called them, almost spitting as he spoke.) Their mood was very dangerous, but fortunately the soldiers dispersed without a riot. On June 4, the Strike Committee announced that it was ceasing the delivery of bread and milk. ("Now they have gone too far!" Father shouted. "These rabble-rousers will have to be stopped. By force if necessary!") Soon, there were stories in the *Free*

Press about infants starving from lack of milk. For the first time since the strike began, the mood of the city seemed be turning against the strikers.

Then, on the evening of June 16, the Mounties swooped down and arrested all ten of the strike leaders. Two days later, the government announced that the leaders would all be held without bail, while they waited for their deportation hearings.

This morning, June 21, six of the ten leaders were granted bail. But the strikers were still very angry and there was now no stopping them. They marched downtown in a huge, silent

Mounties on horseback charge at the strikers. Behind the Mounties marched special constables wielding makeshift billy clubs. And behind the constables came soldiers carrying rifles with fixed bayonets.

At the height of what came to be known as Bloody Saturday a crowd rocked this streetcar off its rails. The strikers viewed every streetcar as a provocation: the streetcar drivers were scabs.

parade to protest the arrests. That's when things turned truly ugly.

Troops of special police on foot and Royal North-West Mounted Police on horseback charged into the silent parade. Many of the police brandished baseball bats and weren't afraid to use them. The strikers fought back, throwing anything they could find, even bricks. They knocked some of the Mounties off their horses, but none of the police seems to have been seriously injured. However, thirty or more strikers were hurt badly, and two men were killed, one of them shot point-blank by a Mountie.

After the strike, Winnipeg returned to normal and its parks and playgrounds to their usual summer uses. Here, a horde of kids streams across the bridge into Assiniboine Park, Winnipeg's biggest.

It was almost midnight before Father arrived home, looking every inch the victorious general. "We have won!" he exulted. "The strikers have been crushed."

I'm afraid that Father is right. For all practical purposes the Winnipeg General Strike is over. But if Father thinks that his workers will return to his foundry and work for him as if nothing has changed, he's lost his mind.

The strike may be over, but I doubt our season of strife has ended. I now understand that the vast majority of those who went out on strike and stayed out for almost six weeks are perfectly good people who simply want to live decent lives. I can't get the young fellow I talked to at the rally out of my mind. Except for the fact his father doesn't own a foundry, he is no better or worse than John or me.

A Woman's Place

Winnipeg after World War I wasn't just a hotbed of labour unrest, it was a centre of the early women's movement. Manitoba was the first province to give women the vote. During the war, many women filled the jobs of the men who'd gone overseas, proving they were perfectly capable of working outside the home.

Canada's most famous crusader for women's rights, Nellie McClung (right), stands with Great Britain's famous suffragette, Emmeline Pankhurst, during Pankhurst's 1914 visit to Winnipeg, where McClung then lived.

When this picture was taken, Emily Carr was an unknown painter who lived alone in a small house in Victoria that was full of pets. By the 1930s she was recognized as a painter who ranked with the famous Group of Seven.

A roomful of women switchboard operators handles calls to Eaton's head office in Toronto. Such clerical jobs increasingly went to women.

In the 1920s, as automobiles became more common, even women began to get behind the wheel, in this case of a Studebaker coupe near Cochrane, Alberta.

Potlatch Village

"THERE IT IS!" I CRIED OUT IN TRIUMPH. THROUGH THE morning mist, the white beach gleamed in summer sunlight, standing out in sharp contrast to the dense, dark green of the forest behind.

"Well done, Christopher!" my father called to me over the throbbing of the boat's ancient engine.

Father had told me that an old Indian village is always marked by its white shell beach. He had visited many such villages, but for me this was the very first time. As we drew closer I could make out the Big Houses and towering totem poles of the ancient settlement I now know by its proper Native name, 'M'imkwamlis, which means "Little Islands Out In Front." But back in the summer of 1923, the year I turned thirteen, I simply called it Potlatch Village. For it was there in December 1921 that Chief Dan Cranmer had held the big potlatch that caused many of his people to be sent to jail. And now we were about to visit the scene of the "crime."

That July visit to these waters was my first trip beyond Vancouver and the Lower Mainland. I had revelled in the voyage by steamer up the coast, stopping at many towns reachable only by water. By the time we'd arrived at Alert Bay, a bustling fishing village off the northeastern coast of Vancouver Island, I felt as though I'd left my other life a thousand miles behind.

At the Alert Bay cannery, we hired a guide who now showed us where to drop anchor off the village and pointed out the rocky islets that gave the place its name. "Those rocks were once the enemies of a great hero," he told us. "He turned them to stone by looking at them, because he wore the skin of a *sisiyutł* he had slain." The *sisiyutł*, my father explained, was a two-headed serpent with great powers. If you looked at one you would die in an instant. But if you killed it, you could acquire its powers for yourself. We rowed ashore in the wooden dinghy. The beach was indeed composed of countless mollusc shells, the leftovers of numberless feasts. We pulled the boat safely above the tideline, then climbed up to

Alert Bay in 1898. Its Native inhabitants, members of the 'Namgis tribe, call it 'Yalis.

the village platform, a sort of main street made of hand-hewn cedar planks in front of the Big Houses that faced the water. Our destination was the house where Chief Cranmer's potlatch had been held. Because it was summertime, we expected to find few people in the village, most having decamped to a summer village closer to their fishing grounds.

Our guide belonged to a group of Natives then commonly known as the Kwakiutl, an Anglicization of Kwagu'ł, the name of one of the local tribes. The people of these parts now prefer to be called Kwakwa̱ka̱'wakw, "the people who speak Kwak'wala." My father was a student of these people.

Outside the Big House, we paused for a moment to breathe in the quietness and beauty of the village. Then we followed our guide into the damp, cool semi-darkness. The only light came from the door behind us and from the smokeholes in the roof, through which brilliant sunshafts entered. Our guide led us to the central fireplace. The mound of ashes had turned green, telling us that many weeks had passed since logs burned here, yet the whole place still held a smoky smell. The high roof, made of planks similar to those that paved the village platform, was supported by four "house posts," whose carved crests told the history of the *numaym*, or group of closely related families, who lived in the house. Around the edges of this great room ran a wooden platform that held partitioned sleeping quarters for the household's high-ranking members. The rest, including all the children, slept in the open spaces. It was hard to understand a world with so little privacy.

For what seemed a very long time we stood silently by the lifeless fire, then our guide started to speak. He told us the story of Chief Cranmer's potlatch, the greatest given in many years among the Kwakwaka'wakw. Chief Cranmer held the potlatch here, away from his home in Alert Bay with its RCMP detachment, because he wanted to avoid trouble. For many years potlatching had been against

Blankets that will be given away as potlatch gifts are piled high in a Big House. The tops of two carved house posts can be seen in the background.

the law, and so in the eyes of the government he was committing a crime, as was each person who attended.

About four hundred people came and the potlatch lasted several days. Many tribes of the Kwakwa̱ka'wakw attended, including a number of important chiefs. Each night there was a great feast – I could almost taste the grilled eulachon (a small oily fish) and the venison stew – and the chiefs and nobles gave many eloquent speeches. Because it was winter, the most sacred time, elaborately costumed dancers wearing beautifully carved masks acted out stories that went back to the beginning of time. In my mind's eye I could see the spirit figures appearing from behind the painted screen stretched between two house posts to dance around the big central fire as the singers narrated the sacred stories.

And, of course, there were many gifts, the greatest gifts for those of the highest rank, but something for every-one. I visualized the blankets piled up almost to the roof of the Big House,

Potlatching

To an outsider, a potlatch would look like a great feast held to celebrate a special occasion, one at which the hosts give away an almost unbelievable number of gifts. But to the Native peoples of the Pacific Northwest, potlatching is an essential part of existence. A potlatch is held to mark every significant life event, ranging from the birth of a child to the raising of a totem pole or the mourning of a death. But it is also the method by which this society establishes a person's status, or importance in the community. The guests at a potlatch thus act as witnesses. By accepting gifts, the guests affirm the host's status. The greater the gifts given, both in quality and quantity, the greater the host's name becomes. And these gifts are much more than blankets or sacks of flour or even pool tables. They include songs, dances, hereditary names, and important ranks such as that of chief.

51

Gifts being displayed at a potlatch at Fort Rupert in 1898.

and all the other potlatch gifts: the sacks of flour, the dugout canoes and motorboats, the trunks and bureaus, the washtubs and basins, the sewing machines and gramophones, and even the two pool tables – special gifts for two of the most important chiefs.

My father had tried to explain the custom of potlatching to me as best he could, though he was quick to point out that no one who has not grown up among the Kwakwa_ka_'wakw will ever understand it fully. But the Canadian government couldn't begin to understand such things. They saw all this dancing and feasting and gift-giving as a form of savagery. And they thought that by banning the potlatch they could force the Kwakwa_ka_'wakw to adopt more "civilized" ways. Instead, the Kwakwa_ka_'wakw kept holding their potlatches, but they held them in secret.

A Kwakwaka'wakw chief holds a copper that he is giving away in honour of his son at a Fort Rupert potlatch in 1894. Of all the potlatch items, a copper carried the greatest value and prestige and gained in value each time it changed hands. To avenge an insult, a chief would break off a piece of a copper and give it to the person who had insulted him.

Dan Cranmer's potlatch, however, was too big to keep secret for long. The government agent in Alert Bay persuaded some of those who were there to testify about it in court. Chief Cranmer and many of those who attended were arrested. He and the others who agreed to give up their potlatch property, including their dancing masks, and to renounce the potlatch were not sent to jail. But those who refused, twenty-two people in all, were sent south to Oakalla Prison Farm with sentences of either two or three months. That was in the spring of 1922.

Now it was a year since the last "criminals" had returned home from jail. Even though I was only thirteen, I remember thinking, "The only crime committed was in arresting these people in the first place."

53

Since that summer day in 1923, I have returned to 'M'imkwamlis many times. For I have followed my father's path and become a student of the Kwakwaka'wakw. As much as any of the peoples of the Northwest Pacific coast, they kept the potlatch alive. In 1951, the Canadian government finally changed the law that had banned the potlatch. Now its dances and ceremonies and gift-giving thrive as part of contemporary Kwakwaka'wakw life. As Agnes Alfred, who attended the 1921 potlatch, said many years later, "When one's heart is glad, he gives away gifts. It was given to us by our Creator, to be our way of doing things, to be our way of rejoicing, we who are Indian. The potlatch was given to us to be our way of expressing joy."

These are some of the dancing masks that were given up by the Kwakwaka'wakw after Dan Cranmer's 1921 potlatch and that became the property of the Department of Indian Affairs. In recent years many have been returned to the Kwakwaka'wakw, and can be seen in the museums at Alert Bay and Cape Mudge.

Strange Rites and Rituals

The potlatch may have looked uncivilized to European eyes, but imagine how strange the ways of white people looked to those who had lived in North America for thousands of years before the first settlers arrived. Here are some of them.

A still photograph from the movie Cameron of the Mounted, *shot in Alberta in the summer of 1920. Only one of these Mounties is kissing a woman. The other three are kissing their horses!*

One of the strangest rituals the settlers brought to Canada was the game of curling, which was invented by the Scots but became far more important here than in the old country. This is a picture of an early Montreal bonspiel.

Imagine trying to explain why this group of Vancouverites would get all dressed up in fancy clothes in order to take a walk across Vancouver's Capilano Canyon.

To Native people, masks had serious ceremonial purposes. Here, an early Toronto photographer has posed a model with a mask because it makes an interesting picture.

The Best Stampede Ever

THAT COULD HAVE BEEN MY MOM ON THE FLYING horse. She's that crazy. When that horse jumped out into thin air, I thought for sure they were both goners – horse *and* rider. But once they took flight, they looked almost like they were floating. So graceful. Time stopped. I gasped – along with about 16,000 other people. I'll bet just about every man, woman, and child stopped breathing. Down, down the horse and rider flew … and then … *SPLASH!* A huge fountain of water shot into the air. The horse had landed in a tank of water that was only ten feet deep. I was sure that both the horse and rider had died.

Then I heard cheers and I saw the rider's head above the crowd. She was standing on her snorting horse, waving and looking about as happy as a cowboy who'd just stayed on top of a bucking Brahma bull for ten whole seconds. But that was the 1925 Calgary Stampede for you. You never knew what to expect.

A trick rider jumps over an Oldsmobile at a Calgary Stampede in the middle of the 1920s.

to make a living as cowboy performers. My grandparents figured that after they got married, they'd settle down. Instead they formed a cowboy act and took it on the road. My dad is a trick rider. One of the finest on either side of the 49th. But a lot of the best riders and ropers at the Stampede are working cowboys who still ride the range the rest of the year. That's part of what makes Calgary so special.

My mother is full of surprises. That's because she's a trick roper and surprise is her calling card. Last year she managed to twirl two ropes at once while riding bareback! She's been riding and roping since she was knee-high to a grasshopper and now she's one of the best riders and ropers you're ever likely to see wearing a skirt.

She and my dad met at a small-town rodeo when they were teenagers. In those days they were both driving their parents right round the bend with the notion that they wanted

My mom and dad are still travelling the cowboy circuit, going to rodeos month in, month out. Since I'm only twelve and have to go to school, I live with my grandparents at their ranch in southern Alberta. My parents visit as often as they can, and at Stampede time we always come up to Calgary for the whole week.

Lucille Mulhall, one of the era's best women steer ropers, has her horse take a bow.

The Calgary Exhibition and Stampede is just about the biggest thing that's ever happened to Calgary, but it started small. Back in the 1880s some local citizens decided that Alberta needed a big annual agricultural fair, and so in 1884 the Calgary Exhibition was born. Only 500 people came, but by 1912, it was the biggest agricultural fair in the Canadian West. That's when a cowboy named Guy Weadick started the Calgary Stampede. After World War I, with more people pouring into Alberta to work in the oil fields, the Stampede grew so fast that

Stampede week ended with a huge street dance on Friday night in downtown Calgary. Even the local merchants dressed up in western costume.

it just made sense to bring the two together. So in 1923 the first-ever Calgary Exhibition and Stampede was held. Since then, it just gets bigger and better every year.

I've never seen this many people on the Victoria Park exhibition grounds. I'd reckon that about twice as many people come to the Stampede as live in the entire city of Calgary. That would make it about 150,000 men, women, and children. But I won't have any trouble getting a seat at the grandstand for the closing night show. There's a section roped off for the families of the performers.

Calgary grew quickly in the 1920s, largely because of the booming Turner Valley oil field nearby, where ten different companies had wells.

59

Royal Winter Fair

If the Calgary Stampede was Canada's biggest rodeo, Toronto's Royal Agricultural Winter Fair was its biggest agricultural fair. The first Royal Winter Fair took place in 1922 and it seems to have gotten better every year since. Toronto city kids have always loved "the Royal," as it has come to be known. For many, it's their only chance to rub shoulders with farmers and farm animals and smell those wonderful barnyard smells. Every kid seems to have a favourite farmyard beast. You'll hear them arguing over which type of cow is best, the enormous black-and-white Holstein or the silver-brown-coloured Brown Swiss, or whether a Cotswold ewe looks prettier than a Leicester ewe. Farm kids love the Royal because it's like a country fair only a hundred times bigger. The most serious young farmers, members of the 4-H club, can enter many competitions. And for horse lovers, the annual horse show in the Coliseum grandstand is a must.

This year my mother is trying out a new rope trick for the act, one that her hero, Florence LaDue, perfected. You do the trick from the saddle, bending over until you're hanging on by the stirrups, and keeping the lariat twirling perfectly in every position.

Just when it looks like my mom's finished her trick – she's back sitting upright and twirling the rope high over her head – my dad comes riding out of nowhere standing on the saddle and lassos her. Somehow – they make it look like she's flying through the air – my mom ends up standing beside him on *his* horse.

Florence LaDue was one of the best trick ropers in the world, as you can see from this photograph of her taken when she was World Champion Lady Fancy Roper.

Chuck wagon Race
Calgary Stampede 1864

The first chuckwagon race was held in 1923 and it quickly became one of the most popular events at the Stampede. Here, two wagons race for the finish line that very first year.

I'm not a bad rider and roper myself. When I grow up, I plan to be a champion lady trick roper, just like my mom. But I'd give anything to drive a chuckwagon in the Cowboys' Chuckwagon Race. Of all the events, it's my favourite.

It's a series of two-wagon races around a full half-mile of the grandstand track. The wagons kick up so much dust that sometimes you can hardly see them, but everybody shouts like crazy anyway. Sometimes when they cross the finish line in front of the grandstand they are still neck and neck. The excitement is almost unbearable. One day I'm going to ride on one of the wagons and hear the crowd cheering me on.

After the show, I hugged my mom and dad goodbye for a really long time before I headed back to the ranch with my grandparents. On the way home, my grandfather told me where the idea for chuckwagon races came from. In the old days, the cowboys spent weeks rounding up the cattle for the winter. They were followed from camp to camp by chuckwagons, heavy horse-drawn carts with round canvas tops that carried food and cooks and stoves. At the end of the fall roundup, when the big workhorses that pulled the chuckwagons realized their driver had turned toward home, they would break into a fast trot. If more than one chuckwagon joined in, they would all soon be racing home at a gallop.

As we drove, I started to chuckle to myself. I suddenly thought of my mom dreaming up a new trick for next year's Calgary Stampede. Maybe she'll lasso a calf from a racing chuckwagon. I wouldn't put it past her.

The long drive home after a day at the Stampede would have taken you through grain and cattle country like this. The taller buildings in the background are grain elevators used for storing harvested grain before it's shipped to market.

U.S.-CANADA BORDER. Sweet Grass, Mont, Coutts, Alberta. Highway No. 91   B-900

Flappers and Jazzers

Rodeo wasn't the only thing that was booming in the 1920s. Everywhere you looked people seemed to be on the move, and often trying something new. Women wore skimpier clothes than ever before, people listened to daring new music, and there were many fads and crazes.

A young woman has her hair curled at a beauty salon. Women's hairstyles changed radically, generally becoming much shorter – and easier to look after. The shortest style was the bob.

These two women enjoying a day at the races at Toronto's Woodbine Racetrack are sporting the latest flapper style. But the true flapper didn't just wear the clothes, she had the strong opinions and the independent mind to match.

The 1920s saw all sorts of fads come and go. One that came and stayed was the bathing beauty contest. These young women are taking part in the 1926 Miss Toronto contest.

The Elk's Band of Winnipeg played a new music called jazz that many people thought shocking. Most shocking of all was the wild way people danced to this new music.

A Visit to Quintland

TODAY IS MAY 28, 1936, THE DIONNE QUINTUPLETS' second birthday, and you're going to Quintland!

You and the rest of your grade eight class have been waiting for this trip for weeks. No, for months. Everybody in the class loves the Quints. They are the first five identical babies in the history of the human race.

Back in September, the whole class started a project about them. Every time the Quints and their bespectacled doctor, Dr. Alan Dafoe, were in a newspaper or magazine, your teacher clipped out the article and put it up on the big Dionne Quintuplets board at the back of the room. That's been just about every day of the week. The Quints are famous. Everyone in the class has written an essay about their favourite Quint. Yours was about Cécile getting her first tooth. Most people can't tell the Quints apart, but you can. Cécile has a way of smiling that's different from the others. Cécile is like the little sister you wish you had. And now you're on a school bus that's taking you to Quintland.

When the bus left Toronto early this morning, you'd never seen the city so quiet. As you rode up Yonge Street, there were quite a few hobos sleeping in doorways or right on the sidewalk. Your teacher, Miss Snelgrove, says these people have lost their jobs because of the Great Depression. She says there are hundreds of thousands of Canadians out of work. Once, when you went shopping downtown with your mom, you saw about

Homelessness could hit anyone during the 1930s. In these days before welfare or unemployment insurance, if you lost your job and your home, you often lost everything. For many, it was difficult to avoid despair.

three hundred people shuffling along in a really long line. Your mom told you they were lining up for something to eat.

This morning, a few of the hobos waved their fists and shouted at the bus, but you couldn't hear what they were saying. Others just sat staring blankly as the bus drove by. Their eyes were scary. Empty-looking. Not like Cécile's eyes. Her eyes are full of life.

A mother and daughter who've just been evicted from their Montreal apartment look sadly at their worldly possessions. Such scenes were all too common in Canada's big cities during the worst days of the Great Depression.

The town of Callander, Ontario, welcomed hordes of visitors after the Quints were born. Their Uncle Léon's gas station, with one pump named for each of the five quintuplets, is on the right.

It has now been about six hours since the bus left Toronto. The Quints live almost all the way to North Bay. Which might as well be the North Pole, it's so far from everything. Miss Snelgrove says that a lot of people in Northern Ontario are French Canadian, like the people in Quebec. Like the Dionnes.

Now the bus is about to make the turn-off to Callander, the closest town to Quintland! "Attention, class. Quiet, please." Everybody is talking excitedly so it takes awhile for Miss Snelgrove to get the bus to calm down.

"Good. We'll be in Quintland in about fifteen minutes. Once we get off the bus, I want everyone to stay with their partner. No running off!"

Just as your teacher finishes, the bus passes under a big archway that says "Welcome to Callander." This is where the Dionne family comes from.

SO YOU WANT A LOVELY COMPLEXION, TOO? WELL, YOU CALLED THE RIGHT NUMBER!

THE DIONNE QUINS give you their "Beauty Secret"

YOU SEE, WE HAVE VERY SENSITIVE SKIN

"If you think *your* complexion is a problem, you ought to hear about ours! For

WE MUST USE THE MOST SOOTHING SOAP

"When we were tiny babies, Dr. Dafoe bathed us only with Olive Oil. So when we were ready for soap and

DR. DAFOE SAID ONLY PALMOLIVE

"Dr. Dafoe chose Palmolive, the soap made with gentle Olive Oil. We're mighty glad he did, for we've never had any complexion trou-

Quint Crazy

After the Dionne Quintuplets were born, the world went Quint crazy. Newspapers and magazines followed their every move, ordinary people collected their pictures, and manufacturers fought over the right to use the Quints, or Quins as they were sometimes called, to help promote their products. Their names and their faces were plastered on everything from cod liver oil to Remington typewriters. You can still find many people who cherish some item of Quint memorabilia, especially the Quint dolls that were sold in the hundreds of thousands. Yet the Quints grew up quite bitter about the way they had been treated – almost like circus animals. In 1998, after many years of seeking compensation, the three surviving quintuplets, Yvonne, Cécile, and Annette, were granted $4 million by the Ontario government, which had made many millions from the tourists who flocked to Quintland.

"There's Dr. Dafoe's house," Miss Snelgrove announces. You can tell that she's also pretty excited. Dr. Dafoe is the doctor who delivered the Quints. He's in charge of looking after them. He's one of the most important people in Canada. "And there's Uncle Léon's Esso station."

Oh, wow! Just like the pictures: five gas pumps, one named for each of the five girls – Emilie, Yvonne, Annette, Marie, and Cécile. The pumps are identical, just like the girls. Cécile's pump is the one in the middle.

Too bad your mom couldn't come on the trip. She loves the Quints almost as much as you do. But she has to go to work every day. Since your dad lost his job, she's the only one earning any money. Your dad says that he's sure "something will come up soon."

Now the bus is jolting along a dirt road full of ruts. It's kicking up so much dust that you almost miss the little sign that says "This way to the Dionne Quintuplets."

"We're almost there!" Miss Snelgrove announces. "Quintland is just over the next hill."

As soon as the gates at Quintland opened, people stampeded to be first in line to see the five baby girls. By the end of the decade, several million people had made the pilgrimage.

And there it is. *QUINTLAND*. The Dionne Homestead is on the right. You recognize it right away. That's where the Quints were actually born. Beyond that are the two souvenir shops run by Oliva and Elzire. (Oliva is the Quints' dad and Elzire is their mom.) The sign reads: *SOUVENIRS – REFRESHMENTS – OPERATED BY THE PARENTS OF THE WORLD'S MOST FAMOUS BABIES.* And there's the Dafoe Nursery where the Quints live!

On the bus, the kids are crowding the windows trying to get a better look. "All right, class. Everybody settle down."

Miss Snelgrove doesn't usually have to talk this loudly.

The bus pulls into the parking lot, which already has at least a hundred cars – more like three hundred – even though it's a weekday.

"We'll unload by rows. Back row first." Two by two by two, you file off the bus. There's a huge lineup of people waiting to get in to see the Quints.

There are quite a few kids in the lineup with their parents. A lot of them must have skipped school. Their parents probably don't have jobs so they can come any time.

69

If you'd had to wait any longer in the hot sun with all those blackflies buzzing around and biting you until you were bleeding around the collar, you'd have started to scream. Or turned into a boiled lobster. Or turned into a screaming boiled lobster!

Finally, the whole class is inside the viewing area. It's like going into a dark, stinky tunnel. The other kids are pushing and shoving. Some of the boys are pinching the girls.

Then you gasp. So does just about every kid in the class. You've seen the Quints a million times in pictures. You wept when they were born. Their tiny, tiny bodies looked more dead than alive. (One of the magazines your teacher read to you in class said they looked like "skinned rabbits.") You've watched them gain weight and start to look healthy. You've got pictures on the class board that show their first steps. You learned about their first words and worried every time they caught a cold.

But this is different. Now you

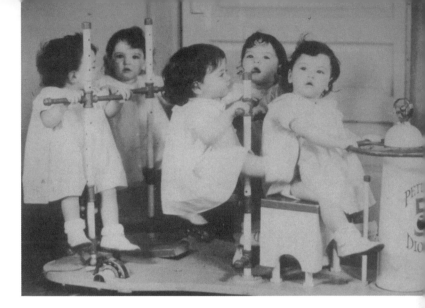

The five girls, age one, take a ride on their personal trolley.

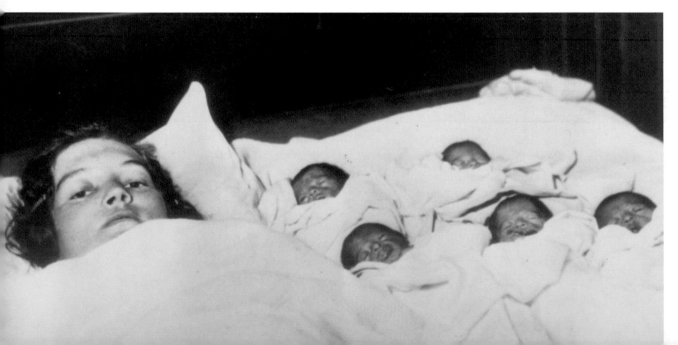

The five infant Dionnes sleep beside their mother Elzire soon after their famous birth on May 28, 1934. The quintuplets were at least two months premature and the largest one weighed barely a kilogram.

are really, truly looking at these five beautiful little girls. Even through the wire mesh screen you can see the Quints' rosy cheeks, their wavy curls of brown hair, and their perfect smiles.

The other kids are whispering to each other, trying to figure out which one is which. But you know which one is Cécile. She's the one playing by herself in the wading pool. Cécile is so beautiful.

Two of the Quints provide some free promotion for the Toronto Maple Leafs.

When Cécile and her sisters grew up, they had mostly bad memories of their childhood. Just look at the expressions on their faces (right) during a visit to New York the summer they turned sixteen. Smiling or not, all five look more sad than happy.

If only you could hold her in your arms and cuddle her. You don't know why, but these kids seem to need more love in their lives. They get the best of everything. They have nurses watching over them twenty-four hours a day. They have the latest toys. But they don't get to see their mom and dad very much, or their five older brothers and sisters. They have each other, but it must be hard for them.

You would give anything to be able to take Cécile home with you. You would love a baby sister to look after. The five beautiful little girls seem happy, but for some reason when you look at them you feel strange. Maybe the word for what you feel is *guilty*. Here you are standing looking at them through a wire mesh almost as if they were in a zoo. Do they even know that you're watching? What will happen to them when they get older and realize that they've been taken away from their family? What will their lives be like once they have to leave the world of Quintland?

Good Times, Bad Times

The Dionne story provided many people with an escape from the tough economic times of the Great Depression. At the Depression's worst, almost two million people out of a population of just over ten million were out of work. And yet many Canadians continued to live happy, ordinary lives.

The prime minister for much of the 1930s was R.B. Bennett, here seen campaigning with his sister. Bennett came into office trying to do something about the bad economy. But nothing he tried seemed to work.

In the prairies, a terrible drought made the bad economic conditions even worse. Several years of scarcely any rain meant that when the wind blew, dust storms like this one could result.

These kids are imitating a Bennett Buggy, a car pulled by an animal because you couldn't afford the gas. The buggy was named for Prime Minister Bennett.

These three women could be Canadians of almost any era, enjoying one of our favourite national pastimes: camping out on Victoria Day weekend.

Off to War

WHEN YOU KISSED YOUR DAD GOODBYE, you could feel the scratchy new wool of his jacket, but you hugged him tight anyway. Your dad looked really handsome in his brand-new Canadian Army uniform. So handsome that he made your mother cry. As he marched down the road in New Westminster, British Columbia, in June 1940, with all the other Canadian soldiers going off to fight the war in Europe, you wanted to hug him one more time. That's why you ran after him.

World War II changed your life forever, just as it changed the life of every child living in Canada. It wasn't just that your dad was gone, although that was part of it. It was also that people at home – including your mom – acted differently. If you were a boy or girl living on Canada's West Coast in 1940, your story of the war might have gone something like this.

After the war began, there were all sorts of shortages that made life on the home front difficult. Because hundreds of thousands of working men had gone to war, many women and retired people took over their jobs – like this man working in a munitions factory (above). Most food staples were rationed, as shown by the sign in this Montreal grocery store window (below).

After your dad marched away, the news of the war got worse and worse. You didn't understand why Canada was fighting the Germans, except that it had something to do with the German leader, a cruel dictator named Adolf Hitler who wanted to conquer the world. By the time your dad reached England, Hitler's army had taken over Holland, Belgium, and France. It looked bad for Great Britain and its allies, including Canada.

At home things went along okay, except that the food got pretty bad. Whenever you complained, your mom reminded you that groceries had to be rationed so that there would be more food for the men overseas. Including your dad. "We all have to do our part," she would say.

And you did your part. Every day after school you and your friends went from door to door collecting scrap metal and used coat hangers for the war effort. Nothing went to waste. Even empty toothpaste containers – in those days they were made of tin, not plastic – were recycled. You considered it your duty. And it made you feel closer to your dad.

But until December 1941, the war seemed very far away. On December 6, the Japanese navy staged a surprise air raid on Pearl Harbor, Hawaii, the head-quarters of the American fleet in the Pacific Ocean. The attack sank most of the warships in the harbour. Fortunately for the Americans, their big aircraft carriers were away at sea. Otherwise, the war in the Pacific might have turned out very differently.

After the Pearl Harbor attack, Japan officially joined the war on the side of Germany and Italy. Canada and the other Allies, including Great Britain and Australia, immediately declared war on

Students at St. Mary's School in North Vancouver practise wearing gas masks in preparation for a Japanese invasion.

A Canadian naval officer questions a Japanese fisherman in Vancouver in February 1942. Soon after the Pearl Harbor attack, the authorities began rounding up people of Japanese descent who lived on the West Coast. Their property was confiscated and they were sent to internment camps. Not until 1988 did the Canadian government apologize to the many thousands of Japanese Canadians who'd had their livelihoods and property unjustly taken away.

Japan. So did the United States, which had stayed out of the war until then.

When Japan became Canada's enemy, your friends at school started to get scared. Japan was a lot closer to Vancouver than Germany. Hawaii was even closer. One of your neighbours dug an air-raid shelter in his backyard. At school, they kept interrupting class for air raid drills. They also made you learn how to wear a gas mask in case the Japanese dropped bombs filled with poison gas on Vancouver. When you put one of the gas masks on, it got very hot inside and it was really hard to breathe. Fortunately, your teacher didn't make the class keep the masks on for long.

Too Funny to Fight

Johnny Wayne and Frank Shuster enlisted in the Canadian infantry in 1941 because they wanted to fight for their country. But the army generals realized these two young men were too valuable to send into combat. They would be much more useful making people laugh.

Wayne and Shuster had been making people laugh since they'd met at Toronto's Harbord Collegiate in the 1930s. By the time they joined the army, they had become a terrific comedy duo. As part of The Army Show *they travelled thousands of miles and entertained hundreds of thousands of Canadian soldiers, putting on funny skits in the midst of war. (In the photograph below, Johnny is pretending to be Hitler by holding a comb above his mouth in imitation of Hitler's moustache. As usual, Frank is playing the straight man.)*

No question about it: Wayne and Shuster were too funny to fight.

At the beginning of 1944, Canadian troops took part in the successful invasion of Italy. Here, Canadian artillerymen are shelling enemy positions near Missoria in Sicily.

The worst part of the war was when one of your friends got a telegram with the black border around the edges, which meant that an older brother or a father had died. After Canada and Great Britain and the United States invaded the Normandy coast of France in 1944, and started to push the Germans back toward Germany, there were a lot of those telegrams. Thousands and thousands of Canadian soldiers died. Was your dad part of the invasion? You had no way of knowing.

You prayed every night that your dad wouldn't have to fight at all, and if he did have to fight that he wouldn't get wounded, and if he got wounded, that he wouldn't get killed. All you knew was that you hadn't had a letter from him in weeks and that the last one came from the big military camp in England where he'd been living ever since he sailed off to war. In one of his letters he'd promised to bring you back a German helmet as a souvenir. He called the Germans "Huns."

Your mom looked really tired, but that was partly because she'd taken a factory job since there weren't enough men to do the work. She looked so exhausted when she got home at night that you felt bad even asking her to help you with your homework.

Many Canadians died during the D-Day landings in June 1944, the biggest seaborne invasion in the history of warfare. This picture shows members of the Ninth Canadian Infantry Brigade wading ashore at Bernières-sur-Mer on the Normandy coast of France.

In the end, your dad was one of the lucky ones. He came home without a scratch – and without that helmet, but you didn't mind. He couldn't believe how much you'd grown. You couldn't believe how much older he looked.

He didn't laugh as much as before. Sometimes you would see him just sitting and staring off into space. But when you asked him what he was thinking about, he wouldn't tell you. "I don't want to talk about it," was all he would say.

A recently returned Canadian soldier (above) *shows three boys how to blow a bugle. A crowd of Dutch civilians* (below) *cheers one of the Canadian soldiers who liberated Holland from the Germans in May 1945.*

After the War

For more than five years, Canada had been at war. Then, in May 1945, the Germans surrendered. In August, after the Americans dropped atomic bombs on Hiroshima and Nagasaki, the Japanese surrendered as well, and hundreds of thousands of Canadian soldiers started coming home.

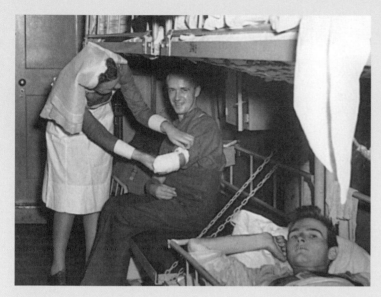

Some war wounds were more visible than others. Here, a nurse aboard a troop ship returning from Europe treats a soldier who has lost part of his left arm. From his smile, we can guess that he's just happy to be alive.

Many Canadian soldiers fell in love while overseas and got married. Here are some of their "war brides," who have just arrived in Halifax in March 1946. Many war brides found it difficult to adjust to life in a strange country.

After the war, the government helped pay the cost of university for returning servicemen and servicewomen, like these ones at the University of British Columbia.

By the end of the decade, Canada was booming. More and more people could afford to buy houses in the burgeoning suburbs, like these two women in Chicoutimi, Quebec.

Hurricane Hazel

TWO DAYS BEFORE THIS PICTURE WAS TAKEN, I DIDN'T even know what the word *hurricane* meant. I sure know now – me and the 680,000 other people who live in Metro Toronto. In September 1954, I'd started working after school as a delivery boy for Mike's Grocery Store. I was eleven years old and it was my first real job. I would never have believed when I began working that me and my dog Curly (I named her that because her hair is so straight) would be making some of my deliveries by boat!

No one who lived through Hurricane Hazel will ever forget it. The people who lost their homes – or worse – probably still get nightmares. My family was one of the lucky ones. When the storm was over, our house was still standing. The headlines in the papers on Monday, October 18 said it all: *FEAR 71 DROWNED, 300 MISSING, CITY BLOCKED OFF*. And the amazing thing is that no one saw it coming.

The rain started last Monday and didn't stop all week. This was pretty unusual for October, but it wasn't like it had never happened before. I still went to school every day. My mother made me wear galoshes, which made me feel really stupid – but they did keep my feet dry. By Friday October 15, when the rain hadn't let up, people were starting to complain. But they weren't too concerned.

Friday, when I got out of school, my mother was waiting for me. She'd taken the bus and then the new subway downtown to go shopping at Eaton's with my little brother Daniel. As the weather got worse she got worried. When we started to walk home, the wind blew even stronger. Pretty soon the rain was blowing sideways, and the raindrops stung our faces like sleet. Suddenly, out of nowhere, a garbage can lid came flying at us! Before I could duck, the lid bounced off the top of my head, then flew away like some crazy metal kite. It didn't hurt much, but my mother looked scared, and Daniel started to cry.

At the corner of our street, Raymore Drive in Etobicoke, there was such a river of

This lunch counter is in Montreal, but it could just as easily be one in Toronto where Daniel and his mom stopped for lunch on the day of the big storm.

This Eaton's store window celebrated the opening of Toronto's new subway in March 1954. Seven months later, some of the new subway was under water.

The Winnipeg Flood

Until Hurricane Hazel, the worst inundation in Canadian history was the Red River flood of 1950. Manitoba's Red River, which flows through Winnipeg, had flooded more than once since the founding of the Red River Colony in 1812. But in 1950, melting snow combined with heavy spring rains caused the Red River to overflow its banks. The nuns pictured below are two of the more than 100,000 people driven from their homes by the flood. "I remember seeing a small cottage floating down the river," one person recalled. "It struck a bridge pillar and the furniture popped out one end as it opened up like a cardboard cereal box." In the flood's wake, the city built massive water diversion channels, but even these couldn't completely stop the flood of 1997, which was one of the worst ever.

water that I wasn't sure we'd make it across. The water was about a foot deep. (So much for those galoshes.) We held hands and waded across.

"I was worried sick about you," my dad said when we slopped in the front door. "The Humber River is rising fast and I want all of you out of here." He looked really upset. "The houses that back onto the river are already partly under water. No telling how high it's going to go. Hurricane Hazel has already caused serious damage in parts of the city."

That's when I first heard the name Hurricane Hazel.

Marilyn's Marathon

In September 1954, only a few weeks before Hurricane Hazel hit, sixteen-year-old Torontonian Marilyn Bell became the first person to swim across Lake Ontario. Her marathon 51.5-kilometre swim from Youngstown, New York, to Toronto took twenty hours and fifty-nine minutes. Marilyn somehow kept going even though she sometimes choked on oil and eels clung to her body. Canadians admired her guts and loved her humble, plainspoken personality. She went on to other famous swims, including the English Channel, but the Lake Ontario swim remained her most memorable.

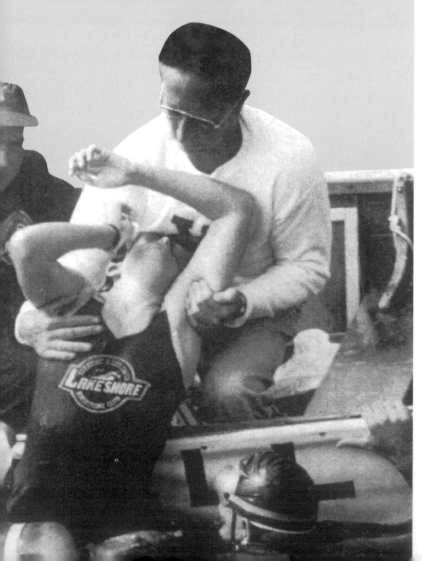

If you were living close to a stream or river on October 15, 1954, you were lucky if your house stayed in one place.

"The safest thing would be for the three of you to go to Aunt Joan's house up on Lawrence. It's higher there and there won't be any flooding. I'm going to stay here and help people get safely out of their houses."

For once I didn't argue with my father, even though I really wanted to stay and help. By the time I'd changed out of my wet clothes and was back downstairs, Dad had our 1953 Chevy warmed up and my mom was in the front seat with Daniel snuggled up beside her. Curly was sitting on her blanket in the back. Flashlights were flickering and the wind carried a few snatches of shouts from the men down the street, but I couldn't really see what was going on. Dad kissed Daniel and my mom, and squeezed my shoulder. Then we drove off.

I still find it hard to believe some of what we saw as we drove. Because of all the water we could only move about one mile an hour up Scarlett Road toward Lawrence. It was more like driving up a river. In some places the water reached almost up to the hubcaps and was leaking in through the car doors. Branches, pieces of shingle, and all sorts of other stuff blew past, some of it bouncing off the car. My mother wasn't saying anything, just staring straight ahead into the driving rain and trying to keep the car on the road. The only way she could be sure we were on the street at all was by lining up with the telephone poles.

By this time, Curly had decided she'd rather sit in the front with me and was huddled in my lap. As we passed one of the poles, the wind snapped the wire in two and sparks started to fly. Then I looked out the window and saw a car that had been washed into a ditch. I began to wonder whether it had been such a good idea to leave home.

This is what cars looked like (above) *during the 1950s. Scenes like this one* (below) *were all too common the day Hurricane Hazel hit. As the floodwaters rose, cars were swept off the streets and into ravines. Houses floated away, never to be seen again. Whole families were lost.*

Somehow we made it to my Aunt Joan's house on Lawrence, just west of Scarlett. There wasn't any flooding there. Her block had lost electricity, so we sat in the dark and talked while the wind howled and the rain lashed against the window. Aunt Joan told us that sections of the new subway had flooded – and that all the trains had stopped running. She'd heard that news on the radio, before the power went out. That and the fact that Hurricane Hazel was being called the worst storm that ever hit Toronto.

I don't remember falling asleep, but when I woke up my dad was there. He'd been up all night, he told us, and things had been pretty awful on Raymore Drive. Several of the houses that had been washed away had taken whole families

Large parts of the countryside around Toronto were devastated. The Holland Marsh looked like it had been hit by a tornado.

Some people spent the entire night on the roof of their house or, as in the case of this family, the top of their mobile home.

The Baby Boom

The kids in this picture, on a visit to Niagara Falls, are part of the baby boom generation. In the 1950s, there was a big increase in the number of children being born in Canada because of all the soldiers who returned from World War II, got married, and started families. And of all the booming cities in North America, Toronto was the boomingest. Its population was the fastest growing on the continent.

The baby boomers are now all old enough to be your parents or grandparents. If they grew up in southern Ontario, they probably have amazing stories about Hurricane Hazel.

with them. People had spent the night trapped in cars and stranded on roofs. One mom and dad had given their four-month-old baby girl to some firemen, but the parents refused to leave their house. Their house was swept away. Now the baby was an orphan.

Around noon, we drove back to our house. It was still standing and looked okay. Down at the bottom of the street, though, everything had just disappeared. All the houses were gone. And many of the people were gone too. People we'd known. My mother wept at what had happened. My father just looked grim. I felt like crying, but I held it in.

These kids look relieved that Hurricane Hazel is over and that life is getting back to normal.

So now I know what a hurricane is. It's a violent, tropical storm that forms over the ocean and hits the coast with winds so strong they can blow your roof off, and drops huge amounts of rain. Once it gets over land, a hurricane usually slows down. But not Hazel – people had never heard of a hurricane that was still so strong this far inland. It wasn't wind that did the damage, though, it was the rain. In just over one day Hurricane Hazel dumped 210 millimetres of rain on Toronto and the surrounding area. All the rain became runoff, and the runoff swelled the rivers so fast that they overflowed their banks.

Thanks to Hurricane Hazel, me and Curly got to deliver bread by boat. It was quite the experience. But I sure hope it never happens again.

Storms of the Fifties

Hurricane Hazel was the biggest real storm of the 1950s, but there were other types of tempests. In hockey, the Montreal Canadiens stormed to five straight Stanley Cups. And television went from being a futuristic contraption to something just about everybody owned.

The most famous hockey player of the 1950s was Montreal's Rocket Richard. As this picture suggests, the Rocket was a fierce and feared competitor. He was the first player to score fifty goals in fifty games.

The hula hoop was one of the biggest fifties fads – although it wasn't ordinarily used as a hoop for the family dog to jump through! Usually, you swivelled the hoop around your waist, trying to see how long you could keep it twirling.

The biggest fifties fad of all was television. Soon Canadians became the world's greatest TV watchers. Today, 98 percent of Canadian households have at least one TV, a world record.

Canada's most popular female athlete in the early fifties was Barbara Ann Scott, who'd won the figure-skating gold medal at the 1948 Winter Olympics.

Fight Over a Flag

"BOY, THIS IS REALLY STUPID!" I THOUGHT TO MYSELF. There I was, on a cool June day standing beside my gran – she always wears such crazy hats – with my dad right behind me and my mom there, too. (As usual, she was talking to her friend, Marge.) It was absolutely the last place in the world I wanted to be right then. All of us – "three generations of Smiths," as my father proudly said – had come from Montreal to Parliament Hill in Ottawa to let Prime Minister Pearson know what we thought about his new flag.

I had never seen my gran so worked up about anything as she was about this flag business. "Mr. Pearson wants to destroy my British heritage," she would say. Or, "My husband William – God rest his soul – fought under the Union Jack in World War I, and your dad, Bill Jr., fought under the Red Ensign in World War II. Those are Canada's flags. We don't need a new one!"

Supporters of a new flag wave the Pearson Pennant at a demonstration on Parliament Hill. Many people thought Prime Minister Pearson's design was perfect, but it wasn't the final choice.

So we'd all trooped up to Ottawa on a June afternoon in 1964, because this was the day Mr. Pearson was going to introduce a bill in the House of Commons calling for a new flag for Canada. We weren't the only people waving flags on Parliament Hill that day. Hundreds of others who agreed with my gran were there as well, waving their Red Ensigns – the red flag with the Union Jack in the upper left corner – but otherwise behaving very politely. "We're not going to be acting like hooligans," my gran had announced in her bossy voice. "Not like some of those New Canadians who think the Red Ensign isn't good enough for them. We will make our point and then we'll go over to the Château Laurier Hotel for a nice cup of tea."

I couldn't help noticing that the other group on the Hill that day, the ones waving flags with three red maple leaves, looked like they were having more fun than the people on our side. (The

Mounties were making sure the two sides didn't get too close.) Most of the maple leaf flag-wavers were a lot younger than my gran. They probably all belonged to what she meant by New Canadians: people who weren't originally from Great Britain. That's where my gran was born. She's English through and through, and hasn't lost her English accent despite having lived in Canada for fifty years.

The red, white, and blue flag was Mr. Pearson's idea of what a "unique" Canadian flag should look like. It had two blue bands and a cluster of three red maple leaves in the middle against a field of white. Mr. Pearson says the three maple leaves are the best symbol for Canada. And the blue bars represent the Atlantic and the Pacific oceans. (The motto of Canada is "From sea unto sea.") Because the maple leaf flag is Mr. Pearson's idea, everyone has been calling it the Pearson Pennant. People have been flying Pearson Pennants from their car aerials, their balconies – some are even wearing them printed on T-shirts. My parents and my gran *hate* Mr. Pearson's flag.

But What Will It Look Like?

While the Flag Debate dragged on in Ottawa, thousands of Canadians (including the ones pictured here) offered their suggestions for a flag design. Some were just plain silly, like the one with a beaver chewing on a birch tree. Some made sense but were too complicated, trying to include every symbol imaginable. At first, many people thought the single red maple leaf flag looked "too plain." But it turned out to be the perfect choice: simple and immediately identifiable even from a distance.

Mr. Pearson's Flag

When Lester Pearson (above) promised Canadians a distinctive flag during the 1963 election campaign, many people thought he was kidding. Or crazy. Why would any politician want to open up such a hornet's nest of emotions and loyalties? But Pearson believed, rightly, that Canada needed a flag that would stand for the whole country, not just its colonial roots. Even when the Flag Debate threatened to drag on forever, he didn't give up. He himself had been a soldier in World War I, so when he went to Winnipeg to speak to a big convention of veterans, most of whom opposed the new flag, they listened. He didn't change many minds, but the former soldiers applauded his courage.

The day that I went with my family to Parliament Hill seemed to last forever – even though I did finally get to eat ice cream while they drank tea at the Château Laurier. But that one long day in Ottawa was like a drag race compared to The Great Flag Debate.

The debate started in June of 1964, and lasted six months. According to my teacher, Miss Szumigalski, during that six months the Members of Parliament gave 308 speeches for, or against, a new flag. Finally, in December, all the parties in the House of Commons agreed to let a committee of MPs make a decision and recommend a flag design. They chose a simpler version of the Pearson Pennant: a single red maple leaf against a white field between two red bars. And that's the one that Parliament was scheduled to formally adopt on February 15, 1965. Which is also the morning that Miss Szumigalski announced that our whole class would have the day off school because we were going to Ottawa to watch Canada's new flag go up the flagpole for the very first time.

Not Ottawa again, I thought.

After being lowered for the last time, Canada's Red Ensign is carried away. A version of it is now the flag of Ontario.

The honour guard stands at attention as Canada's new maple leaf flag goes up the flagpole for the first time.

But this visit wasn't boring at all. Instead of a few hundred people on Parliament Hill, like last time, there were something like ten thousand people. Even though the weather was cold and damp and grey, everyone seemed very excited. An honour guard wearing slate-blue greatcoats and busbies – bearskin hats just like the ones worn by the Grenadier Guards in my gran's pictures of Buckingham Palace – stood proudly at attention at the special flagpole that had been set up in front of the Peace Tower. Everyone was quiet when Mr. Pearson spoke. He had a funny lisp when he talked, but I liked his words. He said, "the fifteenth of February, 1965, will always be remembered as a milestone in Canada's national progress."

A huge crowd gathered on Parliament Hill to see the flag raised for the first time. For people from outside the British Commonwealth the new flag made them feel more at home.

Then an RCMP constable raised the flag up the pole and I got shivers down my spine. It looked good flapping in the breeze. It looked … right.

The next day, Miss S. read us part of an article in the *Ottawa Citizen*, written by a man named Ben Malkin: "There are sometimes fleeting moments when people know that what they are doing, and taking part in, will become recorded history. History then becomes a moment when a man sets foot on an unmapped shore, and records that he has come overland to the Pacific; history is a moment when a boat touches down and opens its ramp on a beach below Dieppe; history is also a moment when a bit of gaily coloured bunting is raised above the Peace Tower on Parliament Hill."

Then Miss Szumigalski said, "Now we have a flag that all Canadians can respect, a symbol to bring us all together." I think Miss S. is right. I guess I'm more of a New Canadian than an old Canadian. (But I'm sure not going to tell my gran!)

Canada's maple leaf flag flies from atop its special flagpole in front of the Peace Tower.

Beatlemania

Kids in the 1960s were a lot more interested in a new rock group from Liverpool, England, called the Beatles than in arguments over Canada's new flag. The Beatles seemed like the most exciting thing ever in the world of music. But they were only the latest in a long line of pop music megastars.

Fans gather at Toronto International Airport to greet the arrival of John, Paul, George, and Ringo. During their first Canadian tour in the summer of 1964, the Beatles played sold-out concerts in Vancouver, Toronto, and Montreal.

Outside Toronto's Maple Leaf Gardens fans wait hopefully for a glimpse of the Fab Four. Inside, the fans screamed their way through the Beatles' entire set. You couldn't hear a word, but no one seemed to care.

These young Beatles fans are wearing their hair in Beatles style, the beginning of the longer hairstyles of the 1960s. Soon young guys were wearing their hair even longer.

Ringo Starr is first down the ramp, followed by John, George, and Paul. The Beatles travelled in a special plane rented for the tour, the first rock group ever to do so.

Grooving at Expo

SO, THERE WE WERE, ME AND MY BEST FRIEND MARTHA, standing in the hot, hot sun in the longest line you've ever seen, waiting to get into the United States pavilion at Expo 67, where I'd told my parents I *definitely* did *not* want to go. When my parents suggested that we drive to Montreal for the Canadian world's fair, where almost every country in the world would be showing off and where there would be gazillions of people, I told them I'd rather stay home in Baltimore with my friends. I thought Canada was a place where it snowed all year round and everybody spoke French. I finally gave in when they said Martha could come with me.

Anyway, so there we were, standing in line for the U.S. pavilion, which is this space-age-looking building called a geodesic dome, and I was starting to think that Expo wasn't so bad. I mean the weather was warm, and everybody seemed to be in such a good mood. And then we met Marc and Pierre.

Thank god my parents let me and Martha go off on our own once we got inside the Expo grounds. After all, we are fifteen. My dad says Canada is completely safe, but we still have to meet them at this weird-looking fountain people call the Artichoke every three hours so they know we're okay.

So there we were, standing in line, when these two guys come up to us and ask us how to get to the Soviet pavilion. I'm sure they just wanted to talk to us, because the Soviet pavilion was about a hundred yards away from where we were standing. Anyway, we started talking and we just hit it off right away. They both have these cute French accents. Pretty soon they were standing in line with us. We must have waited an hour and a half, but Martha and I had such a good time talking to Marc and Pierre that we didn't even notice. They are both really dreamy. But Marc is taller.

A constant stream of people passed through the United States pavilion, one of the most popular at Expo 67. The only people who didn't seem to love it were the Americans, who thought it seemed a bit, well, frivolous.

I'm not patriotic, but I have to admit the U.S. pavilion was pretty groovy. I mean, it was this great big hollow ball made of millions of little glass pyramids. It was designed by some guy named Buckminster Fuller. When you're outside it you could see inside and when you were inside, you could see outside. It was packed with all sorts of wild stuff like this huge picture of Marilyn Monroe and one of Elvis Presley's guitars and a chariot from some movie called *Ben Hur*.

Then Marc and Pierre suggested that we take a ride on the monorail — a train that rides on one rail up on stilts. It goes everywhere on the Expo site, these two islands in the middle of the St. Lawrence River. So they got in line while we went off to meet my parents. We told them that Expo wasn't so bad,

This view of Expo, with a Ferris wheel in the background, looks more like a high-tech carnival than a world exposition.

after all, and that we were finding it very "educational."

From the monorail, Expo 67 could have been a city on another planet. Each building was a vision of the future by a different architect. It looked like the city of tomorrow today.

Marc and I sat together the whole ride. Martha and Pierre sat in front of us. About halfway through Marc put his arm around me.

It was faster to walk than wait in line, but the monorail provided great views of the Expo site and wonderful close-ups of some of its coolest buildings.

103

Canada's Birthday

Canada turned one hundred on July 1, 1967, one of the few days that year when Ottawa was a more exciting place to be than Montreal. The birthday celebrations included a huge birthday cake on Parliament Hill (pictured below). Queen Elizabeth and Prince Philip attended.

But Ottawa's party was only the biggest of countless celebrations that went on in every town and hamlet in the country. In 1967, it seemed that almost every place had its special Centennial project. There were new theatres and arenas, new parks and playgrounds. One town actually built a landing pad for flying saucers – just in case visiting Martians wanted to join the fun.

Habitat 67, a futuristic apartment building designed by Canada's Moshe Safdie, is one of the few Expo structures still standing. And it is still being lived in.

By this time, I was beginning to get why my parents had been so hot to come to Expo. It was simply the coolest, hippest place on the planet. Naturally, Marc and Pierre wanted to see the Quebec pavilion. We liked it okay, especially the forest that was really hundreds and hundreds of cones hanging from the roof reflected in mirrors so that it seemed to go on forever. Then they took us to the Ontario pavilion. Ontario is the province right next door to Quebec, but Marc and

Pierre have never been there! We all thought Ontario's Teen Scene exhibit was pretty groovy. It was this huge room just filled with musical instruments and sports equipment – including hockey sticks and hockey skates, of course – and parts of cars. Everything in it had once belonged to teenagers. The four of us really dug it.

We dug it so much that Martha and I forgot to check the time. Was my dad mad when we showed up at the Artichoke half an hour late! He gave us the usual parent lecture: "Your mother and I were worried sick. We were about to go to security and report you missing." You know the kind of thing. And the usual punishment: "No more going off on your own. You two are sticking to us like glue for the rest of the trip." This was totally and completely awful.

Marc and Pierre were waiting for us *right now* in the lineup at the Russian pavilion. I was sure they'd be so mad that they probably wouldn't show up at the hotel later, like they'd promised. I didn't know what I'd do if I never saw Marc again.

The Soviet pavilion couldn't have been more different from that of its American arch-rivals. The American pavilion was lighthearted; the Soviet pavilion was serious and meant to impress the world with its technological prowess.

All through supper I was so tense that I could hardly eat. My mom and dad were really tired so they decided to go to bed early. We told them we would just stay in our room and watch TV. We left the TV on when we snuck down to the lobby around 9 p.m.

No sign of Marc and Pierre, so we waited. I could hardly breathe. They showed up after about half an hour. Marc gave me his gap-toothed smile and this big hug. I was so relieved and so happy to see him. Then they took us on

Visitors to Expo were also impressed by Montreal's vibrant downtown (above) *with its many restaurants and varied nightlife. A more restful spot was the giant geometric fir tree in the Community pavilion* (below).

106

a tour of the city. There were *soooo* many people on the streets, I couldn't believe it. Not like Baltimore. Nobody goes downtown in Baltimore after dark.

We sat in a sidewalk café and Marc and Pierre both ordered beers. That would never happen in Baltimore if you were only seventeen. Marc offered me a sip. It tasted really bitter.

When the guys brought us back to the hotel, Marc kissed me for the first time. That night I hardly slept at all.

The next morning I sweet-talked my dad into letting us go off on our own. (I can almost always get him to forgive me.) Marc and Pierre were waiting for us at the Community pavilion. The part of the pavilion I liked best was the tower in the middle that was supposed to look like a gigantic fir tree from British Columbia. Before I came here I'd never even heard of British Columbia. Marc explained to me that it's like California, only colder. Marc and I held hands and looked up into the tower for a long time. Next summer he and Pierre are going to hitchhike all the way to the west coast of Canada. I'm going with them.

Vive le Québec Libre

During the summer of Expo, everybody in Montreal was in a great mood until July 24, the day Charles de Gaulle came to town. The French president shocked most people when he stood on the balcony of Montreal City Hall and said, "Vive le Québec! Vive le Québec libre!" People were so shocked because de Gaulle was openly supporting the cause of Quebec separatism, which had become a hot issue in the 1960s. More and more Quebeckers were starting to believe that their province needed to become more independent from the rest of Canada. Some even believed it should become a totally separate country. So de Gaulle's words, spoken in the middle of a birthday bash that made Canada look good to the outside world, couldn't have come at a worse moment.

It was beyond awful saying goodbye to Marc. We met him and Pierre at a record store near the hotel. I started crying and then his eyes got watery, which made me cry even more. Martha, who has a boyfriend back home in Baltimore, finally pulled me away. She knew my parents would be going bananas because we'd disappeared.

This time my father was so angry he wasn't even speaking to me. I felt like sobbing the whole way home but I couldn't because I didn't want my mom and dad to know about Marc. So I just sat in the back and stared out the window. I didn't even talk to Martha.

Marc and I are going to write each other every day. And I'm coming back to Montreal to go to college – there's an English university called McGill. And to think I never wanted to come to Expo 67 in the first place. The drive home to Baltimore took forever.

These performers participated in the Centennial birthday party on Parliament Hill on July 1, 1967.

Those Wild Sixties

Expo 67 may have been one big party, but it couldn't last forever. The 1960s was a decade of conflicts and contradictions. Many kids rejected their parents' values and dropped out to join something called "the counterculture." Yet at the same time, many Canadians continued to live just as they had in the 1950s.

Sometimes the protests of the sixties brought older and younger people together, but more often they did not. One issue that really divided the generations was the war in Vietnam, which many Canadians believed to be unjust.

These young people are attending a "love-in" in Montreal's Fletcher's Field. Some of them are probably hippies who have rejected everything about the world of their parents, above all its concern with hard work and making lots of money.

In the 1960s artists experimented with all sorts of different forms and styles. Here Canadian artist Michael Snow sits in his New York studio next to his sculpture Walking Woman.

One thing that stayed the same was the long-running television show Front Page Challenge, where mystery guests (in this case Malcolm X) tried to stump a celebrity panel.

Guns in October

M Y OLDER BROTHER, JEAN, IS A SEPARATIST – an *indépendantiste*. He believes that Quebec must become a separate country to achieve its true identity. I am not so sure. I've listened to what Pierre Trudeau has to say. I think he is not only very handsome (for a politician), but very smart. Prime Minister Trudeau is a strong federalist, which means that he believes Canada must remain one country. But it's hard to argue with my brother. He's so sure of himself. And I love him a lot.

Last St-Jean-Baptiste Day, Jean joined the big parade in Montreal. Saint John the Baptist is the patron saint of Quebec and his *fête* is always held on June 24. After the parade, Jean got a little carried away: he jumped into a fountain and started waving our flag, the beautiful blue-and-white flag of Quebec.

French Connection

You're probably wondering what a picture of a king and queen is doing in a chapter about the October Crisis of 1970. The connection has to do with Quebec's strong sense of its history. The picture was taken in 1908, during the celebrations marking the tercentenary of the founding of New France in 1608. It shows two people from Quebec City, identified only as Monsieur A. Couillard and Madame Auguste Carrier, dressed up as King Henri IV of France and his wife, Queen Marie. Henri IV was the French king when Samuel de Champlain founded the first permanent colony in what is now Quebec. The fleurs-de-lys on his royal robes are emblems of the French monarchy. They also appear on the flag of Quebec.

Police examine the scene of one of the early explosions engineered by the Front de Libération du Québec, while a crowd watches from a distance.

I can hear you asking the question: Why would Quebec want to separate from Canada? Isn't Canada a great country? My brother explains it to me this way: "We have never been treated as equals in Canada. Ever since the British conquered us, we have been second-class citizens, even in Quebec. It is time to take control of our own destiny. We must protect our French language and our French culture. We are a nation. Now we must become our own country."

Jean spends a lot of time reading about politics and about revolutionaries. He is a great admirer of Che Guevara, who helped Fidel Castro win the Cuban revolution, then died fighting with rebels in the jungles of Bolivia. Jean says that the Front de Libération du Québec, the FLQ, wants to start a revolution here.

No one had even heard of the FLQ back in 1963, when they first started putting bombs in mail-boxes in the English neighbourhoods. Everybody has heard of them now. Since 1963, they have stolen all sorts of explosives from the Canadian military and exploded something like two hundred bombs.

Back in 1968, when the FLQ blew up a bomb at the residence of our mayor, Jean Drapeau, my brother said Drapeau had it coming for being a collaborator with the Anglos. (If anyone had been hurt, I am sure he would have spoken differently.) I don't argue with him. After all he is nineteen, four years older than I. He goes to university, the Université de Montréal, where he studies *les sciences politiques*. To me, politics is not a science. It is all about emotion.

During the October Crisis, any Montrealer who looked slightly suspicious risked being stopped and questioned, possibly jailed. These students could easily have been targets.

No one had ever seen anything like it: Canadian troops patrolling the streets of Canadian cities. Kids (above) are playing in a park in Ottawa while soldiers stand guard. The soldiers would stay for weeks, until the crisis was over. These kids (below) seem more curious than concerned about the soldiers guarding this building in downtown Montreal.

What emotions did I experience on October 5, 1970, the day of the first kidnapping? Astonishment? Yes. Fear? Definitely. That morning at 8:30, an FLQ cell abducted James Cross, the British trade commissioner in Montreal. (A cell is a secret group of revolutionaries who communicate only with each other and live in hiding.) To me, James Cross seemed like someone of no importance. But Jean said he was a symbol: of British conquest, of English-Canadian domination. I had no idea that the event would lead to chaos – to helicopters landing in city streets, to tanks rolling up onto people's front lawns, to random searches by the police. To what people will now always refer to as the October Crisis.

From the moment James Cross was kidnapped, Jean began behaving strangely. He came home very late from the university. We hardly saw him. The day the FLQ manifesto was broadcast over the radio – this was the only one of the kidnappers' demands that the

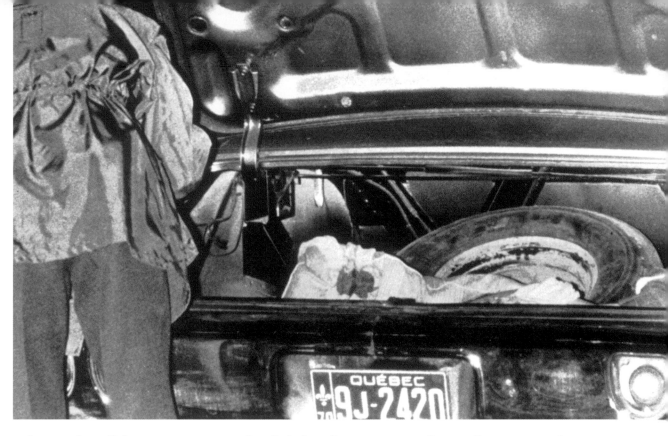

On October 17, the body of strangled Quebec justice minister, Pierre Laporte, was found in the trunk of a car in St. Hubert, Quebec. After Laporte's murder, public sympathy for the FLQ evaporated.

government agreed to – he did not come home at all. *Maman*, of course, was very worried. So was I.

Jean finally appeared the next morning and slept all day. Then, on October 10, he disappeared completely. This was the day we heard the news that Pierre Laporte had also been kidnapped. Laporte was the Quebec minister of labour. He was one of our own.

Jean is so headstrong, but I didn't believe he would do something foolish. He loved to sit in the student centre and talk politics with his friends, but that was all. Talk. We didn't see Jean for seven days. Later he told me that he

had joined a group of students at the Université who claimed they had formed their own cell of the FLQ. When the revolution started, they would be ready. They slept in an old warehouse down by the harbour. Mostly they talked and drank coffee and listened to the radio.

Jean came home the night of October 17, after Pierre Laporte's body was found in the trunk of a car. As soon as Jean's "cell" heard the news, it dispersed. I think they all went home to their mothers. By this time the soldiers had already started arresting people. I have never seen him so frightened.

At Laporte's funeral in Montreal on October 21, Trudeau (centre) *looked nothing like a man in charge. He and Premier Bourassa* (at far right) *were deeply shocked by the murder.*

With all the troops moving through the city, we felt like we were living in an occupied country. After Laporte was killed, the soldiers were everywhere. Jean never left his room. But I think the men in power were almost as frightened as was my Jean.

That Pierre Trudeau, when he was asked how far he would go to stop the FLQ kidnappers, he said, "Just watch me." I still like him, but I could see that although he was talking tough, he was scared, too. He brought in martial law

– the War Measures Act –

because of *two* kidnappings. These are not the actions of a man who is cool under pressure. And don't talk to me about Robert Bourassa, our *premier ministre*. Bourassa is very weak. He let Trudeau take over.

For my family, the worst moment of the October Crisis was when the Montreal police came knocking at our door. It was so early in the morning that we were all still in bed. Papa answered the knocking. When he asked the officers for their warrant, they told him they didn't need one. "This is a war," they said. They pushed past him and up the stairs. A few minutes later they came down with Jean in handcuffs.

During the crisis, policemen in riot gear became a familiar sight on the streets of Montreal.

Pallbearers carry Pierre Laporte's coffin, draped in the Quebec flag, into Montreal's Notre Dame church for the funeral mass. On December 3, the other kidnap victim, James Cross, was released unharmed.

While Jean was in jail, the rest of my family went to the funeral of Pierre Laporte. There were many others who came to pay their respects. This was a very sad day in the history of Quebec.

They let Jean out of jail in December, after the first kidnappers released James Cross. The kidnappers had made a deal: a military airplane took them to Cuba. Good riddance, I say. In the end, Jean was not charged with anything. The same with most of the other five hundred people they arrested during the "state of emergency."

Why did they pick on Jean? you ask. Someone had informed the police about his so-called cell. Every one of his political friends was picked up. And every one of them was freed without any charges.

Christmas that year was very strange. No one felt like exchanging presents or eating much. Only *Maman* went to Mass on Christmas Eve.

On December 28, François Simard, Paul Rose (left), and his brother Jacques (right), the three men suspected of kidnapping and murdering Pierre Laporte, were captured in a tunnel under a farmhouse outside of Montreal.

After Jean came back from jail he looked like a ghost. He'd lost weight. The little potbelly he'd been starting to worry about was gone. And he looked much, much older. Worst of all, he was quiet all the time. Three days after Christmas, we were all sitting around watching television – some silly Hollywood movie from the 1940s that we'd put on for Papa. For once, we didn't mind. Then the announcer broke in to say that the murderers of Pierre Laporte had been arrested. They had been hiding beneath a farmhouse south of the city. The October Crisis was over.

Maybe. Since then, people here are talking differently. They are very mad at Trudeau for arresting all those people for no reason. They are listening more carefully to René Lévesque and his Parti Québécois. He is no revolutionary, M. Lévesque. But he does believe we must become a country of our own. After what happened last October, I'm beginning to think he may have a point, but I have not decided. I will wait and see.

The Masks of Trudeau

During the October Crisis, Canadians saw a very different, more serious Pierre Trudeau than the stylish, fun-loving guy they'd voted for two years earlier. Over the years they would learn that Trudeau had many masks. But love him or hate him, they couldn't take their eyes off him.

Of all Trudeau's faces, the only one that was collectible was the one that appeared on the face of this watch created as part of the wave of Trudeaumania during the 1968 election campaign.

Trudeau entered office a bachelor. Before he married the much younger Margaret Sinclair in 1971, he dated various women. Here he dances at a costume ball with an unidentified partner.

Trudeau liked to appear unconventional, as when he executed a pirouette behind Queen Elizabeth's back. Actually, he rehearsed it beforehand.

During the 1968 election campaign Canadians treated Trudeau as if he were some brainy rock star. Huge crowds came out to hear him speak everywhere he went.

Canada Wins!

HOW DID YOU FEEL WHEN PAUL HENDERSON SCORED? On top of the world. As good as Henderson? Nobody could feel that good. The school cafeteria went crazy. People were shouting and whooping and screaming and jumping on tables. Even the teachers had lost it. Some of the kids were banging the chairs against the tables like war drums. The principal started leading the chant: "Go Canada, Go! Go Canada, Go! Go Canada, Go!" In no time, everybody joined in.

You'd hardly been able to see the game, the TV set was so far away, but it didn't really matter. One little TV screen for the whole school. Even in colour it was hard to tell Team Canada from the Soviets. God, how you hated the Russians. They stood for everything bad in the world. And Team Canada, they stood for everything good: for freedom and democracy – everything your parents had worked so hard for since coming to Canada before you were born.

An election rally in Vancouver's Chinatown a few years after the 1972 Summit Series brings out a traditional Chinese dragon. Vancouver has one of the largest Asian populations in North America.

When you told your dad that you wanted to play in the NHL one day, he looked at you like someone from another planet. "Do you think this is why your mom and I work seven days a week?" he asked. "So you can play games for the rest of your life?"

Of course, he didn't say the words in English. Even after twenty years in Canada, living in downtown Vancouver, he spoke hardly any English. In Chinatown you didn't have to. The language he spoke was Cantonese, the kind of Chinese they speak in and around the city of Canton, in southern China. But language didn't stop him from building a good life for you and your brother and your two sisters. Everywhere in the shop that's also your apartment on Pender Street there were bean sprouts growing. On the tables, in the bathtub. Your parents supplied bean sprouts to all the best Chinese restaurants and Chinese groceries in Vancouver.

When you tried out for the school hockey team, your dad just didn't understand. But he let you do it because it was a Canadian thing to do. And he wanted all of you to fit in. When you made the team he was proud. He'd never played any sport in his life – when would he have had the time? But he and your mom even came to some of the games – when they could get away from work, which wasn't often.

In September 1972, at the beginning of the Canada-Soviet Summit Series – the biggest hockey series ever – you'd announced you wanted to be only the second person of Chinese descent ever to play in the NHL. (The first was Larry Kwong, who played in the 1940s.)

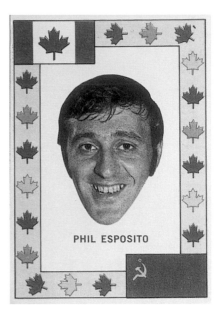

Special hockey cards (right) were issued for the first Canada-Russia series. After it was over, the only card worth as much as Paul Henderson's was Phil Esposito's. Players on the Soviet bench (below left) watch intently as the first game gets underway.

PHIL ESPOSITO

The series began in Montreal on September 2. As far as you could tell, everybody in Canada was watching that first game. In Vancouver, people left work early so they could be home in time for the 5:00 p.m. start. All the guys on the team said they were confident that Canada would win the series in eight games straight, but you could tell they were nervous, just like you. Nobody knew what to expect from the Russians because they'd never competed against the best players in the world, the Canadians in the National Hockey League. Still, there was no way the Russians were going to beat a team that had players like Ken Dryden, Phil Esposito, and Bobby Clarke.

You watched Game One with your best friend from the team, Nick Artemakis. His family is from Greece and his father was just as weirded out when Nick joined the team as yours was. To Nick's dad there was only one sport, soccer. But Nick wanted to play hockey.

Game One started out just like everybody expected. Espo – that's Phil Esposito – scored after only thirty seconds. Six minutes later Paul Henderson scored again. Canada was ahead 2 – 0 and it looked like they were going to wipe the

The Soviet and Canadian teams line up for the national anthems before Game Three, which was played in Winnipeg.

floor with those Russians. But then something went wrong. The longer you watched, the sicker you felt in your stomach. The Soviets started to skate faster than the Canadians. They skated circles around them, passing the puck better than you'd ever seen anybody do. They scored one goal and then another. At the end of the first period the game was tied.

It just got worse after that. Team Canada managed to score only one more goal. The Russians scored five. They won the game 7 – 3. More awful, they made the Canadians look bad. It was embarrassing. Humiliating. You felt like dying. So did Nick.

Kids like these young hockey players idolized the NHLers on Team Canada and were sure they couldn't possibly lose.

At school the next day, the team got together at recess to talk about the game. The guys were pretty upset. But you all agreed that Canada would come back in Game Two. Then win the series. How could Canada lose to the stupid Red Russians?

The Canadians did win Game Two in Toronto – they fought like it was the Stanley Cup finals and they won 4–1, but that was the last game they won in Canada. Game Three was a tie and Game Four, in Vancouver … well, you didn't even want to think about it. When the Vancouver fans started to boo Team Canada in the third period it was just too gruesome. You and Nick turned off the TV

Two Soviet players hug in celebration of yet another goal against Canada.

and went outside to practise shooting with a stick and a tennis ball. Canada lost that game 4–1.

Serge Savard (left) *and Bill White* (right) *in action against the Soviets' Alexandr Yakushev.*

So, by the time the series moved to Russia, no one was predicting a Canadian victory. The Soviets had won two of the four games in Canada and tied one game. Now the rest of the games would be played in Moscow, in front of Russian fans on Russian ice.

Team Canada played really well in the first game in Russia, but they still lost. There was no way they could win now.

Team Canada goaltender Ken Dryden and his wife (right foreground) take in the sights of Moscow's Red Square during the Russian half of the Summit Series.

But people still watched the games – hoping for a miracle.

Canada won Game Six, but it still looked impossible. Then they won Game Seven, and you started to believe. In those games Henderson was unbelievable. You'd never seen anyone play so well. So when it came down to Game Eight, the final game that would decide the series, the principal decided to cancel morning classes so the whole school could watch. Everyone knew a tie wasn't good enough. If Canada tied, the series would end in a tie. Only if Canada won the game could they win the series.

Paul Henderson (centre) was always in the thick of the action and scored an amazing number of important goals, including the series winner.

Watching that game was tenser than anything you'd ever felt. When the Soviets scored first, everyone in the school cafeteria booed. It was almost like being at a real game in a real rink. Then Canada tied and the cheering practically took the roof off. Then the Soviets went ahead again – and even though you booed as loudly as anyone, you got that sinking feeling you'd had in Game One. At the end of the second period, the Soviets were ahead 5 – 3. How could Team Canada come back now?

When the third period began, good old Espo – who's almost as good as Bobby Orr – went out and scored to make it 5 – 4. Nick punched you

harder than usual, he was so happy, but you barely felt it. Then speedy Yvan Cournoyer scored a real beauty. *BUT THE GOAL LIGHT DIDN'T GO ON!* You were furious. So was everyone in the caf. People were shouting, they were so mad, "Kill the Ref! Kill the Ref!" There was some kind of big fight going on in Moscow between the Canadian officials and the Russian officials. You couldn't really tell what was happening, but when it was over, Cournoyer's goal counted! Canada and Russia were tied with only seven minutes to go.

By the final few games in Russia, the tension was almost unbearable. Here, Phil Esposito chews out a Soviet player who obviously doesn't understand a word he's saying.

With less than a minute to play, and the score still tied, Paul Henderson is on the ice with Esposito and Cournoyer. In the Soviet end, the puck comes out to Espo, who takes a shot. The Soviet goalie stops it easily, but it bounces out to Henderson all alone in front of the net. He shoots and the goalie stops it again, but it comes back out to him. Henderson whacks at the rebound, and shoots it toward the net, a slider that doesn't seem to stand a chance. He scores! Canada wins!

Later, your dad admitted that he'd turned on the TV set at home during the final period. So he saw Paul Henderson score the greatest goal in the history of hockey. Your dad even admitted that he cheered out loud. In Cantonese. But he understood every word of the play-by-play from some guy named Foster Hewitt: "Here's a shot … Henderson made a wild stab for it and fell … Here's another shot! Right in front! They score! Henderson has scored for Canada!"

Paul Henderson raises his arms in victory after scoring the winning goal in Game Eight of the Canada-Soviet Summit Series. With less than a minute to go, Henderson yelled from the bench for Pete Mahovlich to get off the ice so he could come on. Pete obliged. And the rest is history.

Different Faces

During the 1970s, Canadians became more and more aware that they lived in a country of many peoples and many cultures. As a result, the biggest cities became much more exciting places to live. And the faces that appeared in books, newspapers, and on television began to reflect Canada's growing diversity.

The photos on this page were taken by John Reeves as part of Canada's celebration of International Women's Year in 1975. This picture is of Vancouver homemaker Betty Lee.

One of the most influential women in Canada was Barbara Frum, who hosted the hugely popular CBC radio program As It Happens. Frum would later become the host of the network's television newsmagazine, The Journal.

Rosemary Brown was one of the few black women ever elected to Parliament and a staunch crusader for social justice. She almost won the NDP leadership in 1975.

This picture gives no hint of the depth and passion of Margaret Laurence's novels, including The Stone Angel. She often wrote about characters who were outsiders.

Terry and Me

IT WAS JUST AFTER 7:00 A.M. ON MAY 1, 1980, WHEN I SAW him coming toward me. All alone except for a van following along maybe a hundred metres behind. At first I thought he was skipping. But as I got closer, I could see that he had one real leg and one fake one. He was "running" down the Trans-Canada Highway in the middle of nowhere – also known as Corner Brook, Newfoundland – and he only had one leg. Creepy.

I was on my bike as usual. It was early morning – my favourite time to ride – before school, when there's nobody on the road except a few big trucks. I slowed down when I got close to him. He was hop-skipping along and panting and his expression was the way you look when something hurts. His fake leg made a kind of clicking sound as he moved. At first he didn't seem to see me. But then the guy driving the van tooted his horn and the runner looked me straight in the eye. I rode away as fast as I could.

Terry never made it to this prairie stretch of the Trans-Canada Highway, but he saw many vistas this empty.

skateboard? When I'm on wheels, I'm happy. Riding my bike, I just let my wheels carry me – up and down the hills around Corner Brook. Which is on the west coast of the island of Newfoundland. Just water and rocks and trees and mountains. When I'm on my bike or my board, my problems evaporate. Like a thick fog burned off by a hot sun.

On my way back into town I passed him again, but this time I didn't slow down. All the way to school, I couldn't get that runner out of my head. What on earth would move a guy to run down the Trans-Canada Highway when he had only one leg? Then I began to wonder about the leg. Where did the real leg end and the fake one start? How did he attach it to his body? Did it hurt? How badly? And what had happened to his real leg?

I couldn't imagine not having a leg. How would I ride my bike? How would I

My mom and dad say I spend way too much time on my bike and my board. They say I should spend more time doing my homework. I'm in grade eight, but I should be in grade nine. My dad says that if I don't "pull up my socks"

In the 1980s, skateboarding was really big. This kid jumping over a pile of skateboards might be practising for a skateboarding championship.

132

I'll end up like him, stuck working at the pulp and paper mill. My dad used to be a fisherman, but he lost his boat when the cod started to run out. He misses the sea. He loved being a fisherman.

When I got to school on this particular morning there was this huge banner over the front door that read, "All Hallow School Welcomes Terry Fox." When we all marched into the auditorium for assembly, I looked up and saw the runner with the fake leg standing on the stage beside the principal. He looked my way and gave me a wink. I looked at my feet. When the principal introduced him, he said the runner's name was Terry Fox. He had left St. John's, Newfoundland, on April 12 on his Marathon of Hope to raise money for cancer research. He was going to run from St. John's to Vancouver, British Columbia. On one good leg. The other leg had been amputated after he got cancer. He was twenty-one years old.

Then Terry gave a speech. He talked about the need to raise money for cancer. When he said, "I bet some of you feel sorry for me," I looked up. "Well,

don't," he went on. "Having an artificial leg has its advantages. I've broken my right knee several times and it doesn't hurt a bit." Everyone laughed.

After school, I hopped on my bike and headed south. I was some distance out of town before I caught sight of him about half a kilometre away, just like this morning, hop-skipping along the highway with the van close behind.

By the time of Terry's marathon, Newfoundland fishers like this one were worried about keeping their way of life.

This biker (above) is probably about the age of the kid in this story. Terry (right) takes a break during one of his long days on the road. Here, he's sitting in the front seat of the van, checking out his progress on a map.

Then I heard a big truck roaring up behind me, coming from Corner Brook way. Another semi was barrelling up from the south, from the direction of Port-aux-Basques. Trying to make it home to St. John's before bedtime, no doubt. Neither one of them was giving an inch. They met smack-dab where I was riding. I dove for the ditch. I heard the trucks blast their horns, and felt a rush of wind in my hair as I lay there in the gravel.

My leg was hurting and when I felt my cheek my hand came away bloody.

It seemed like forever until I heard someone shout, "Are you okay, man?" It was the driver of Terry Fox's van. He and Terry arrived at almost the same moment. They helped me into the van and onto a cot. They gave me an ice pack for my knee – it would hardly bend – and bandaged the cut on my cheek. They said they'd take me home.

Doug, the driver, loaded my bike in the van – it didn't seem too damaged – and we headed back into town. Terry sat with me in the back and we talked. Just like we'd known each other all our lives. He asked me about school and stuff. I asked him about Vancouver.

Then he asked, "Wouldn't you like to see my leg?" At first I thought he was joking. But he wasn't. "Sure," I said.

So he took it off and handed it to me. I could see that his stump was black and blue and that it had blisters. It must have hurt a lot when he ran. It must have taken a lot of courage to try to run. The artificial leg was amazingly light. After I'd had a good look, I handed it back to him.

Terry Fox addresses the huge crowd that came out to meet him in Nathan Phillips Square in front of Toronto City Hall in early July. One of Terry's sports heroes, Darryl Sittler, the captain of the Toronto Maple Leafs, told the crowd that Terry was the real superstar and gave him his 1980 NHL all-star team sweater.

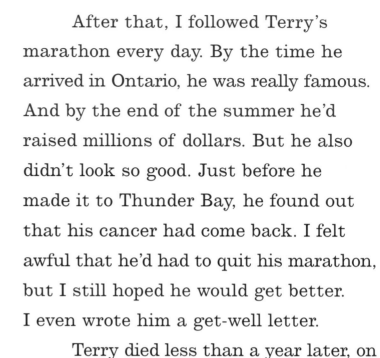

After that, I followed Terry's marathon every day. By the time he arrived in Ontario, he was really famous. And by the end of the summer he'd raised millions of dollars. But he also didn't look so good. Just before he made it to Thunder Bay, he found out that his cancer had come back. I felt awful that he'd had to quit his marathon, but I still hoped he would get better. I even wrote him a get-well letter.

Terry died less than a year later, on June 28, 1981. I got up and spoke at the special memorial assembly at school. I told the story of how Terry had helped me when he didn't know me from Adam. Afterwards we had a special campaign and raised more money for Terry. Just about every kid contributed.

So Terry Fox never did finish his marathon. He only made it about half-way. Or did he? By the time he died he'd raised over $24 million, so he'd reached his goal of raising as many dollars as there were people living in Canada in 1980. And his run had inspired just about the whole country. I'd say he made it, and then some.

Terry Fox as he looked during his Marathon of Hope.

Other Marathons

Terry Fox's Marathon of Hope was only one of many causes that Canadians supported during the 1980s. As the country's population grew and the cities became more crowded, people became concerned about pollution and other environmental issues, such as acid rain.

This picture shows part of the old-growth forest in the Clayoquot Sound area on the west coast of Vancouver Island. In the 1980s, many Canadians protested the way the big forest companies were "clear-cutting" this ancient forest.

Another big issue in the 1980s was pollution, including acid rain. Big power plants and nickel smelters release chemical gases into the air. When these chemicals fall as part of rainwater it's called acid rain, and can kill fish in many lakes.

In 1983 the Canadian government decided to allow the American armed forces to test cruise missiles in northern Alberta. The decision outraged many Canadians.

In the 1980s the blue box for recycling became a common sight in Canada, as people realized that something had to be done to reduce the amount of garbage.

137

Trouble at Oka

T HE MAN ABOUT TO PUNCH OUT A CANADIAN SOLDIER is someone I know. He isn't ordinarily a violent person. But by the date of this photograph, September 18, 1990, he had become very angry and was prepared to fight – if he had to. He and many others in my community were set to defend our rights, and to protect the land that had been taken away from us. If I had been older, I would have been ready to fight, too.

I am a Mohawk and I live in a place called Kanesatake on the north shore of the St. Lawrence River just west of Montreal. I live here with my mother and my two younger brothers. (My dad died three years ago, when I was ten.) Nearby is the town of Oka, where mostly white people live. Usually the Indians and the white people keep to themselves and get along okay. But from early July until late September 1990 the town of Oka, Quebec, became a war zone.

At the barricade, with the flag of the Mohawk Warriors.

to remember. The pines look down on a traditional Mohawk cemetery that is right next to the nine-hole golf course that belongs to the town of Oka. My father is buried in this cemetery beside his father and his grandfather.

Like many of our Mohawk men, my dad was an ironworker. Mohawk men are fearless about heights and are the best at working the high steel when a tall building is being built. But even the best sometimes slip and fall. My dad was one of the best. When I am in the Pines I can feel his presence. I know he would have been one of those who built the first barricade when the town of Oka tried to take over more of our traditional land.

In the spring of 1990, the mayor of Oka announced that the town had decided to add nine holes to the golf course. They were planning to make a

Once a month my family goes to a clearing in a special place called the Pines to burn tobacco in my father's memory and offer up prayers to the Creator. The tall, straight pine trees that give the place its name were planted more than a hundred years ago by our people, and we consider the clearing sacred. It is here that we come as a community to celebrate and pray. And

lot of money by selling the land next to it to developers who wanted to put up expensive houses alongside. But building the new nine holes meant bulldozing the Pines and surrounding the Mohawk cemetery with the golf course. That's when my mother and many others in Kanesatake, including the Mohawk Warriors, decided something had to be done. That's when they built the first barricade, a log barrier across the dirt road that leads to the Pines.

When school finished in June we camped out with my mom in the Pines along with many others. Defending the Pines had become a community event, and there were whole families living in tents pitched in the clearing. Both the town and the Quebec government tried to talk us into taking down the barricade. Then, on July 10, a judge ordered the barricade removed. The next day, the mayor of Oka called in the Quebec provincial police, the Sûreté du Québec, or SQ.

This young man at the barricade outside of Oka is one of the Mohawks who called themselves warriors and were prepared to fight with the police, or the Army, if necessary.

The sign in the photo reads: "These lands are under the native sovereignty of The Mohawk People of Kanesatake so respect the natural beauty of The Land for The future generation"

On the morning of July 11 I woke up very early, just when the first light was filtering through the canvas walls of our tent. My mom's sleeping bag was empty, but my brothers Samuel and Jacob were still asleep. I could smell the bacon and eggs my mom was cooking for our breakfast. I lay there listening to the birds singing.

Suddenly my mom was inside the tent pulling us out of our sleeping bags. "The SQ are here!" she said anxiously. "Get dressed quickly. Miriam, help your brothers."

Samuel and Jacob had never dressed so fast. Outside the tent, I couldn't believe what was happening. Beyond the barricade there must have been about fifty police, some of them in riot gear. They wore dark jumpsuits and bullet-proof vests and carried big rifles. Some climbed up into trees. Others got down into ditches and pointed their guns at the barricade. Some hid behind their police cars, with the lights still flashing.

Then I saw my mom walking with the other women. There were about a dozen of them altogether, walking arm in arm right up to the police with their helmets and shields and guns. The women carried nothing to defend themselves. In traditional Mohawk society, the women are the guardians of the land. My mother is one of our spokespeople. When no man came forward, the police got very impatient, so they lobbed some canisters of tear gas toward the women. I saw my mother choking and rubbing her eyes as the women retreated.

After the first tear gas attack, the police tried to persuade the women

After the police used tear gas on July 11, some of the people at the Oka barricade began wearing gas masks whenever they expected another attack.

142

These are some of the Mohawk women who were gassed by the Quebec police on July 11, 1990.

to surrender. No way, my mom and the others told them. This is Mohawk land and we will defend it with our lives.

Then the police started firing more tear gas shells, and people started to run for cover. But for some reason I just stood there, clutching Samuel and Jacob close. The cloud of tear gas surrounded us and we started choking. Samuel and Jacob were screaming when my mom reached us and pushed us to the ground. She lay on top of us and covered our mouths and eyes with wet handkerchiefs, but the tear gas still stung something awful.

No one agrees about what happened next, except that shots were fired. Did the police shoot first? Or the Mohawks? Nobody knows, but one of the bullets hit one of the policemen, Corporal Marcel LeMay, as he was running for cover. He was thirty-one years old and had a two-year-old daughter and another baby on the way. To this day, no one is sure whether Corporal LeMay was killed by a bullet from a Mohawk gun or from a police gun. But either way, I don't think his life was worth adding an extra nine holes to a golf course.

After Corporal LeMay was shot, the police retreated. Then one of the Warriors who'd been hiding in the forest came out and got into an abandoned police car. He drove it into the Pines with the siren going. People were cheering. Another Warrior climbed up into the front-end loader the police had brought to take down our barricade. Instead, he used it to build a new one, right across Highway 344. Part of the new barricade was a crushed police car. I was excited when all this was happening, but also really scared.

When the SQ came back, they built their own barricade at the bottom of the hill on the Oka side of our new barricade. And that's when the stand-off began: the Kanesatake Mohawk behind their barricade and the Sûreté du Québec behind theirs. My mom said it was too dangerous for us to stay in the Pines, so we went back to our house in the village. But every day we came to watch. That was how we spent the summer: watching and waiting for something bad to happen.

The stand-off between the Kanesatake Mohawks and the SQ went on for weeks and weeks and weeks. First Nations people from all across the country – not just Mohawks – came to

After one of the Mohawks hijacked the front-end loader, three others rode victorious in its shovel.

After the Canadian Army moved in, the village of Kanesatake was surrounded by soldiers and razor wire.

Oka to help. At Kahnawake, the closest Mohawk reserve, just across the St. Lawrence River, some Mohawks barricaded the Mercier Bridge, which thousands of Montrealers cross every day when they drive to and from work. The Kahnawake Mohawks were trying to divide the SQ so they wouldn't attack the Oka barricade in force. The bridge blockade got a lot of white people very angry, but the worst was when a group of them stoned some Mohawks trying to leave Kahnawake. (One of them later died of a heart attack.)

In late August, Robert Bourassa, the premier of Quebec, called in the Canadian Army. A few days later, the trucks and jeeps and armoured personnel carriers moved in. The soldiers, dressed for combat, unwound rolls and rolls of razor wire. The Army used many tricks, including sending a helicopter flying low over Kanesatake to wake us up in the middle of the night or to scare us during the day. By the end of the month, people were getting pretty frazzled. My mom stayed calm and helped others to calm down. But the negotiations went nowhere. And the Army had us completely surrounded.

Finally, near the end of September, the Army announced that it was going to pull out if the Warriors didn't give up their weapons and surrender. That night there were long discussions about what we should do. In the end, most people agreed that it was better to move our fight to a different arena than to face off against the SQ, who were surely looking to avenge the death of Corporal LeMay. On September 26, we let the Army take down the barricade.

My mom says the stand-off was worth it, because we turned the eyes of the whole world on Oka and we stood up for our rights. We are still waiting for our claim on our traditional lands to be recognized, but at least there won't be a golf course any time soon. The Canadian government bought the land – our land – from the town of Oka.

The events at Oka in the summer of 1990 have made me a different person. I can't forget the razor wire that surrounded us or the soldiers with their guns or the armoured personnel carriers. It is much harder now for me to believe in Canadian justice and Canadian democracy.

Outsiders may criticize those of us who stood together, but I know that my father would have been very proud.

This young boy, named Aniatariio, was one of the children who lived through the Oka Crisis.

146

First Nations Rising

The Oka stand-off became an important symbol for First Nations people across Canada, after many often-fruitless years of struggle. These days, Native Canadians are taking more and more control over their own lives, in ways that include various forms of self-government.

This famous picture was taken by American filmmaker Robert Flaherty for his 1922 documentary, Nanook of the North. It's an example of the romantic view of Native people held by many non-Natives.

These two elderly Cree saw their world transformed in the 1970s after Hydro-Québec began building its massive James Bay hydroelectric project, which went ahead despite Native protests.

Native member of the Manitoba legislature, Elijah Harper, raises his fist after helping kill the Meech Lake Constitutional Accord, which did not address Native concerns.

This igloo is being built for the April 1, 1999, ceremonies to mark the creation of the territory of Nunavut, Canada's first political unit controlled by First Nations people.

Millennium Trip

12/31/99

12:00 p.m

ARE YOU ONLINE?

Yup.

Did you see any fireworks?

What, are you kidding? In nowhereland rural Ontario? Just saw the TV ones – from Ottawa.

Hey, sorry I asked!! From our balcony I can see the fireworks in Sir Winston Churchill Square. They're awesome.

Rub it in. Wish I could be in Edmonton with you right now.

Yeah. I'm dying to see you. I can't believe we've been chatting for a year and we still don't know what each other looks like.

Major drag. What about your Internet camera?

If I could only get it to wrk...

Did you download the driver I told you about?

Yeah, but these things are tricky.

Hey, if you get it working we'll be able to meet.

Visually.

A virtual trip!

Are your parents home tonight?

Is Perth County the armpit of the planet?

How come? Y2K impaired?

Sort of. Didn't I ever tell you what happened to us during the ice storm?

Ice storm?

Of Jan 98. Stopped eastern Ontario and Quebec cold.

Laughing Out Loud.

LOL. But it sure wasn't funny at the time.

Do tell.

We were driving to visit my grandparents in the Eastern Townships.

Sounds like something from Anne of Green Gables.

Close. Farm country south of the St. Lawrence.

We made it as far as Sherbrooke, no problem, but that was all on the autoroute. Whch they'd been salting all day. Only a few big rigs

in the ditch. Just past Sherbrooke is where we take our trn-off.

So?????

My dad didn't slow down enough on the exit ramp. Car went into a skid, then started to spin, a full 360.

Geez.

We ended up upside down in a ditch,

This ice-covered mailbox was just one of the casualties of the terrible ice storm that hit the north-eastern part of North America in January 1998. The storm was the worst anyone could remember.

hanging by our seatbelts.

Geez. Was anybody hurt?

Not a scratch on any of us.

Cool.

Cold. We managed to get out of the belts, but there was no place to go, we just sat on the floor – which was really the ceiling – and waited. And froze.

I wish I could have been there to rescue you!

My hero! A cop finally found us. Nice guy, even if he didn't speak much English. Never been so friggin cold in my life. Thought we were gonna die.

That's what ya get for using twentieth century transportation!

That's why my parents are home tonight. Thanks to the ice storm of 98, they've got the millennium bug real bad.

Not my folks. They've been snoozing in front of the TV since 9.

Snore.

What are your folks doing now?

Still sitting in the kitchen by the wood stove, where they've been since 10, listening to the radio, drinking coffee (like they need it, they're so pumped), waiting for news of Y2K disaster.

Fewer than a hundred years ago, automobiles like the one above were still competing with horse-drawn buggies – and often losing! Throughout the century Canadians faced disasters of both natural and human origin, like the fire that gutted Winnipeg's Kelly Block (below) in January 1911.

In the fall of 1999, worried citizens (above) stocked up on water and other necessities in anticipation of Y2K catastrophe. Their fears proved unfounded. But early immigrants travelling from Europe to the Canadian West (below), needed to carry everything they could to their new homes.

How nineteenth century.

Exactly. The way my dad has this place stockpiled with wood he's chopped and canned goods and extra blankets, we could be on the TV show Pioneer, *or something.*

BTW, Did I ever tell you my great grandparents were pioneers? Real ones?

Give me a break!

No seriously. Came to Canada by boat from Poland in 1905. Took the train from Quebec to Saskatoon. Settled near a little place called Rosetown. Cleared a farm, built a sod house.

A what?

Sod house. Bricks were made of sod.

Seriously?

My gran has shown me pictures.

I wouldn't put a dog in one.

Spking of hounds, how's Molly Brown?

Asleep on my bed, of course.

Yellow labs are such peple persons!

I'm dying to meet her.

I may just about have the camera working. Been tinkering while we've been chatting.

Make sure you unzip the driver file.

Works better when it's not compressed!

Roger.

I'll bet your great grandparents would roll over in their graves if they heard a girl talking geek speak!

Very funny.

You have a beautiful mind.

Give me a break Leonardo.

I hope you don't mean diCaprio?

Da Vinci, darling.

I was getting that sinking feeling!

LOL.

LOL.

I've been thinking.

Me too...

Um, what I meant was, you know how everyone's been making such a big thing about it being the end of the century and the start of a new millennium and all that crap.

Totally.

I've been wondering why everyone has been going on and on about the twentieth century. Like it was something special or something.

Only century they've got, I guess.

Anyway, at Christmas I was talking to my grandparents about what life was like before television.

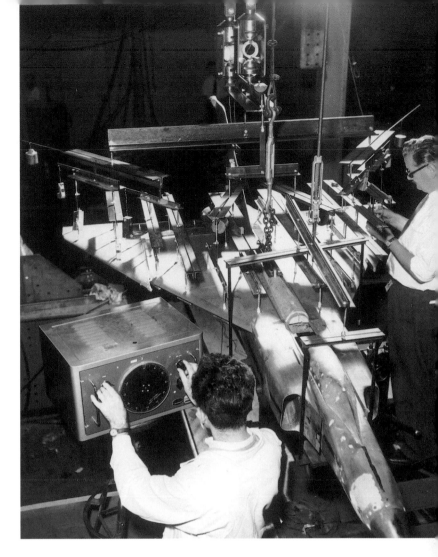

At the beginning of the century, Canadians, including the four men below, were still learning how to fly. By the 1960s, the Canadian aircraft designers who created the Avro Arrow (seen above being tested as a scale model) were among the best in the world.

Who knows what this person is thinking as he or she looks into the future. One thing's for sure, however. The twenty-first century will come up with at least as many unexpected twists and turns as did the twentieth.

During the Dark Ages.

My gran says they used tog et together and play, like, piano, harmonica, guitar, whatever, and sing.

Wouldn't it be the best to visit them back … uh, when was it?

1930s. The swing era. Big Bands, baby.

Yeah, I'd love toe be able to drop in on my parents or their grandparents when they were like, fifteen.

As long as we didn't have to live in one of those sod huts!

Exactly. Drop in, not hang around.

If you could pick one decade to visit, which one would it be?

The sixties. That's when my mom and dad were kids, and the way they talk about it, it was just the best time ever. There's this photo of my dad when he was our age, with hair down to his shoulders. He looks really dumb.

Me, I'd go all the way back to the beginning of the century. I'd be an invisible fly on the ship that brought my great-grandparents to Canada.

Good thinking. Flies don't get seasick!

Hold on, I think I've got the camera working.

No, really?

One moment please.

I've waited this long.

OK, I've unzipped the driver and run the .exe file. What now?

Well, if everything's working right, just run the video chat software. I don't know what it's called on your computer.

Face to Face. I think it's working. Is yours clicked on?

Yup.

Prepare yourself to see one handsome dude.

My heart is pounding.

Here's the moment you've been waiting for!

You didn't tell me you were such a dog.

LOL. That's Molly Brown. But you look

really nice.

They call me Sheena, Queen of the Perth County Jungle.

Growl.

Okay, shy boy, show me your real face.

Just as I expected. Kinda cute.

Aw, shucks. Now if we could just touch.

Sorry, I haven't downloaded the software.

It hasn't been invented yet.

But it will be!

In the 21st century.

Our century.

Index

Photo Sources

Every effort has been made to contact copyright holders. In the event of omission or error, the editor should be notified at Otherwise Inc., 356A Queen Street West, Toronto, Ontario, Canada M5V 2A2.

Some agency and archive names have been abbreviated in this source list:

AMNH: American Museum of Natural History
AO: Archives of Ontario
BBS: Bruce Bennett Studios
CMCP: Canadian Museum of Contemporary Photography
CO: Collection of Otherwise Inc.
CP: Canadian Press
CTA: City of Toronto Archives
HHOF: Hockey Hall of Fame
NAC: National Archives of Canada
PAA: Provincial Archives of Alberta
PABC: Provincial Archives of British Columbia
PAM: Provincial Archives of Manitoba
PANS: Provincial Archives of Nova Scotia
QNA: Quebec National Archives
SAB: Saskatchewan Archives Board
TFF: Terry Fox Foundation
TRL: Toronto Reference Library
VPL: Vancouver Public Library

Front matter
p.i Story time in Newfoundland: CMCP; p.iii Swim class: NAC PA61387; p.v Dancing class: PAM; p.10 Family in wheatfield: NAC; p.14-15 Boys on beach: CTA.

Starting Over
p.16 Immigrants on ship: NAC; p.18 Street scene: Notman Archives/McCord Museum of Canadian History; Immigrant family: NAC-PA 10254; p.19 Mailbox: Glenbow NA-1758-14; Train interior: SAB R-B3275-2; p.20 Wheatfield: PAA B 273; Man at door: NAC C 5093; p.21 Pioneer house: SAB S-A 129; p.22 Bridge construction: NAC-PA 08759; Family scene: CO; p.23 Horses and ice: PAM N-3212; Collapsed bridge: NAC-C 09766; p.24 School house: CO; p.25 Klondike men: NAC-C 16460; Boat to Klondike: CO; Gold bars: NAC-C 1283; Panning for gold: Glenbow NA-1786-8.

The Day the World Ended
p.26 Kids in hospital: CTA-James Collection; p.28 Halifax family: CO; Halifax Citadel: CO; p.29 Flattened landscape: CTA-James Collection SC 244-2435; Teacups: CTA-James Collection SC 244-4; p.30 Flattened city: CO; p.31 Boat: PANS N-138; p.32 Rescued: CTA SC 244-8198; p.33 Boy in bed: CTA-James Collection; Nuclear explosion: NAC-PA 115124; p.34 Coffins: CTA-James Collection SC 244-2456; p.35 Going over the top: NAC-PA 648; Billy Bishop: NAC-PA 1675; Loading munitions: AO 4424; Man washing face: NAC-PA 1193.

Revolution in Winnipeg
p.36 Horses approaching streetcars: PAM Winnipeg Strike 28; p.38 Girls in class: PAM N2684, Foote Collection 1584; Girl and two maids: PAM N231; p.39 Boy scouts: SAB R-B8132-48; p.40 Winnipeg rally: PAM N2736, Foote coll. 1670; p.41 Anti-strike rally: PAM N2742; I'd hate like hell to be a scab: CTA SC 244-2543; p.42 Crowd of strikers: PAM; Horses on street: PAM C-26782; p.43 Streetcar on side; CTA-James Collection 2543, PAM; p.44 Kids on bridge: PAM N2258, Foote Collection 1337; p.45 Nellie McClung: Glenbow C-6-1746; Emily Carr: PABC 51747; Women with phones: AO 2487; Woman driving car: Glenbow NA 1019-68.

Potlatch Village
p.46 Totem poles: CO; p.48-9 Alert Bay: AMNH; p.50 Blanket stacks: AMNH; p.51 Potlatch detail: AMNH; p.52 Potlatch: AMNH; p.53 Man and Boy: AMNH 106707; p.54 Masks: PABC PN11637; p.55 Cameron of the Mounted: Whyte Museum of the Canadian Rockies; Curling: NAC; Capilano Canyon: City of Vancouver Archives; Woman and Mask: NAC PA112013.

The Best Stampede Ever
p.56 Diving horse: Glenbow NB-16-417; p.58 Horse jumping car: CO; Miss Lucille Mulhall: Glenbow NA-3985-6; p.59 Oil field: Galt Archives P19760211091-GP; Dancing on street: Glenbow NA-1644-25; p.60 Royal Winter Fair: TRL p.58; Florence LaDue: Glenbow NA 628-4; p.61 Chuck wagons: Glenbow NA-446-93; p.62 Alberta Road: CO; p.63 Woman at beauty salon: OA/Eaton's Archives; Flappers: CTA-James Collection SC 244-579; Beauty contest: CTA SC 244-1028; Jazzers: PAM N1888, Foote Collection 288.

A Visit to Quintland
p.64 Dr. Dafoe and Quints: CO; p.66 Montreal eviction: NAC-C 30811; Man on sidewalk: NAC-PA 56874; Food line-up: NAC-C 30564; p.67 Welcome to Callander: CO; p.68 Lovely complexion: CO; p.69 Crowd at Quintland: CO; p.70 Quints and mom: NAC-PA 133266; p.68 Quints on toy car: CO; p.71 Quints playing hockey: CO; p.72 Miss Cecile: CO; Teenage Dionnes: CTA SC 244-2166; p.73 Bennetts in car: NAC-C 21528; Dust Storm: PAA/A-3742; Kids in cart: CO; Girls camping: PAM N3040, Foote Collection 2415.

Off to War
p.74 Boy and soldiers: NAC-C 38723; p.76 Munitions man: NAC-PA 116363; Food rations: NAC-PA 108300; p.77 Naval officer and Japanese man: NAC-PA 112539; Kids in gas masks: VPL 44965; p.78 Wayne and Shuster: NAC-PA 152119; Firing shells: NAC-PA 151748; p.79 D-Day Landing: NAC-PA 137013; p.80 Soldier and boys: NAC-PA 117889; Soldier and Dutch crowd: NAC-PA 134376; p.81 War wounded: NAC; War brides and children: PANS; Students: NAC-PA 116069; Ladies in Chicoutimi: QNA E6,S7,P90-59.

Hurricane Hazel
p.82 Boy delivering bread: CTA SC 257-1993; p.84 Lunch counter: CMCP; p.85 Progress in better living: AO 4471; Rowing nuns: PAM N16103; p.86 Marilyn Bell: CO; House on side: CTA; p.87 Car on road: CO; Car on side, CTA; p.88 Destroyed Houses: CTA SC257-2011;

p.89 People on trailer: York University/Telegram Collection; Baby boom family: CO; p.90 Ring of boys: TRL; p.91 Rocket Richard: HHOF; Hula hoop: NAC-PA 124855; Women watching TV: NAC PA 172794; Barbara Scott: CO.

Fight Over a Flag
p.92 People waving flags: CMCP; p.94 Men and flags: CMCP; p.95 Boy with green and white flag: NAC; Three men and flag: NAC; p.96 Lester Pearson: NAC; p.97 Flag descending: NAC; Flag raising: NAC; Crowd at flag raising: NAC; p.98 Flag flying: NAC; p.99 Beatles fans with signs: CMCP; Fans wearing shorts: CMCP; Mop tops: CMCP; Beatles arriving in Canada: CMCP.

Grooving at Expo
p.100 United States pavilion: George S. Zimbel; p.102 Escalator in United States pavilion: TRL; p.103 Monorail: NAC PA-169833; Ferris wheel: TRL; p.104 Centennial cake: NAC; Habitat 67: TRL; p.105 Soviet Pavilion: CMCP; p.106 Downtown Montreal: Sam Tata; Fir tree in Community pavilion: TRL; p.107 Charles de Gaulle: NAC PA117531; p.108 Centennial celebration on Parliament Hill: NAC; p.109 Protestors: NAC; Hippies at Fletcher's Field: NAC; Michael Snow in studio: CMCP; Front Page Challenge: CBC Collection.

Guns in October
p.110 Man in fountain: Gabor Szilasi; p.112 King and Queen: NAC PA-024125; Explosion: NAC PA 115131; pg.113 Student protesters: NAC PA-139982; p.114 Soldiers in park: NAC; Kids and helicopter: NAC PA-129838; p.115 Body in trunk: CP; p.116 Trudeau at Laporte funeral: NAC PA-151863; Montreal Police: NAC PA-137167; p.115 Laporte funeral: NAC; p.118 Jacques and Paul Rose: CP; p.119 Trudeau watch: TRL; Trudeau in mask: CP; p.117 Pirouette: CP; Trudeau shaking hands: PABC.

Canada Wins!
p.120 Kids cheering: CP; p.122 Vancouver parade: NAC; p.123 Russian hockey team: HHOF; Hockey card: CO; p.124 Boys in hockey uniforms: CMCP; Beginning of game: Brian Pickell; p.125 Soviets celebrate: Brian Pickell; Soviets play: Brian Pickell; p.126 Dryden in Moscow: BBS; p.127 Hooking: BBS; Phil Esposito and Soviet player: Denis Brodeur; p.128 Henderson scores: IHF; p.129 Betty Lee: CMCP; Barbara Frum: CMCP; Rosemary Brown: CMCP; Margaret Laurence: CMCP.

Terry and Me
p.130 Morning Run: CP; p.132 Trans-Canada Highway: Derek Shapton; Skateboarder: CP; p.133 Fisherman: CMCP; p.134 Boy on bike: CMCP; p.132 Terry Fox in van: *Toronto Star*; p.135 Terry Fox at Toronto City Hall: CP; p.136 Terry Fox running: Sports Hall of Fame; p.137 Rainforest: Adrian Dorst; Pollution: NAC; Cruise Missile: NAC; Recycling: NAC.

Trouble at Oka
p.138 Oka fight: CP; p.140 Oka barricade: CMCP; p.141 Mohawk prepared to fight: CMCP; p.142 Mohawk in gas mask: CP; p.143 Women in truck: *Montreal Gazette*; p.144 Front-end loader:

Montreal Gazette; p.145 Canadian Army moves in: CMCP; p.146 Aniatariio: *Montreal Gazette*; p. 147 *Nanook of the North*: NAC; Native Canadians at James Bay: NAC; Elijah Harper: CP; Nunavut preparations: CO.

Millennium Trip
p.148 Fireworks: CP; p.150 Icestorm: CO; p.151 Car falling off bridge: CTA SC 244-63; Fire at Kelly Block in Winnipeg: Foote Collection, PAM; p.152 Preparing for Y2K; Pioneer family arriving in Quebec: NAC C5611; p.153 Avro Arrow testing: NAC PA203474; Early flight: NAC PA60831; p. 154 Walking in field: Bryce Duffy.

Sources photo
p.159 "Bicycle Bill": Foote Collection, PAM.

Final photo
p.160 Story telling: NAC PA 67288.